PRAISE FOR *NAIL IT!*

Pat Williams nails down the top ten list for job interviews, but in doing so, he also hits on the head many of the best pieces of advice for living a life of integrity and success. I use many of his chapter subjects in my own speeches about leadership and accountability. Reading this book will help anyone shine during these tough economic times when jobs are few and candidates are many.

—JOHN C. HITT, *President, University of Central Florida*

I have known Pat Williams for many years and I consider him one of the best business minds around. His new book, *Nail It!*, will help all job-seekers to think of themselves as multi-functional Swiss Army knives.

—ANDY DOLICH, *COO, San Francisco 49ers*

Pat Williams has produced a book that is required reading for anyone seeking a job in today's market. *Nail It!* gives you a complete game plan for interview preparation and execution. With Pat's "nail gun" in your hands you will be well positioned to succeed.

—BILL POLIAN, *President, Indianapolis Colts*

Wonderfully practical advice for not only nailing the job interview but also making sure that it's the right job for you!

—PATRICK T. HARKER, *President, University of Delaware*

Nail It! is a textbook on how to nail your job search. It's a classic read for a tough job market.

—JERRY REINSDORF, *Owner, Chicago White Sox and Chicago Bulls*

Pat has been picking winners for a long time. His insights are clear and constructive. Follow them and you are on your way.

—RANDY LEVINE, *President, New York Yankeess*

Capitalizing on his decades of experience and achievement in professional sports, Pat Williams offers a winning formula for those seeking employment in the most competitive of job markets.

—ADAM SILVER, *Deputy Commissioner, National Basketball Association*

Once again, Pat Williams has "nailed it." If there is a must book out there in this day and age, this is it! Thoughtfully written and amazingly candid, *Nail It* has something for everyone, first job or last.

—JIM LIVENGOOD, *Athletic Director, University of Arizona*

This book gives you a thorough look at the job search and interview process that we all confront at one time or another. Pat Williams offers a comprehensive set of practical suggestions and common sense principles that will help you successfully navigate that process.

—LARRY LUCCHINO, *President and CEO, Boston Red Sox*

This is the book everyone wished they had read before interviewing for the job that got away. Fantastic insights, suggestions and directions from one of the great authorities of "people culture" and human behavior.

—DR. BILL SUTTON, *Co-author of* Sport Marketing, *Consultant and Professor, DeVos Sports Business Program, University of Central Florida*

Pat Williams gives common sense advice, as he always does, about one of the most pivotal times in any of our lives. It's a series of light bulbs that go off in your head as Pat illuminates your path to success. A great read for those preparing for an interview, and, by the way, for those of us doing the interviewing, as well.

—TOM WILSON, *President, Palace Sports & Entertainment, Inc., President, Detroit Pistons*

In typical Pat Williams' fashion, *Nail It!* captures the essentials of the job search, the job interview process and of being the successful hire in a competitive market. Pat's writing has the trademark energy, enthusiasm, and insight that have made him successful in his work and in his life. A good read for anyone of any age.

—PAT O'CONNER, *President, Minor League Baseball*

An NBA executive & father of nineteen shares insights

NAIL IT!

guaranteed to help you become any team's "first-round draft pick"

10 Secrets for Winning the Job Interview

Pat Williams

CO-FOUNDER OF THE NBA'S ORLANDO MAGIC

with Peggy Matthews Rose

Published by Advantage, Charleston, South Carolina.
Member of Advantage Media Group.

ADVANTAGE is a registered trademark and the Advantage colophon is a trademark of Advantage Media Group, Inc.

Printed in the United States of America.

ISBN: 978-1-59932-158-5
LCCN: 2009936096

This publication is designed to provide accurate and authoritative information in regard to the subject matter covered. It is sold with the understanding that the publisher is not engaged in rendering legal, accounting, or other professional services. If legal advice or other expert assistance is required, the services of a competent professional person should be sought.

Most Advantage Media Group titles are available at special quantity discounts for bulk purchases for sales promotions, premiums, fundraising, and educational use. Special versions or book excerpts can also be created to fit specific needs.

For more information, please write: Special Markets, Advantage Media Group, P.O. Box 272, Charleston, SC 29402 or call 1.866.775.1696.

Visit us online at **advantagefamily**.com

This book is dedicated to Audra Hollifield and Lorisse Garcia, two remarkable women who have anchored the Orlando Magic human resources department for years and impacted many lives along the way. They live and breathe the material in this book every day. It's a privilege for me to witness them in action.

—PAT WILLIAMS

CONTENTS

INTRODUCTION: Why You Need to Read This Book—*Right Now!*.....8

CHAPTER 1: Network...11

CHAPTER 2: Be Interview Question-Ready..........................25

CHAPTER 3: Be Prepared...35

CHAPTER 4: Display Professionalism...................................56

CHAPTER 5: Exude Self-Confidence......................................66

CHAPTER 6: Exhibit Communication Skills.........................75

CHAPTER 7: Radiate Energy and Enthusiasm...................100

CHAPTER 8: Reveal Your Extraversion...............................110

CHAPTER 9: Have Integrity...118

CHAPTER 10: Reveal Creativity..130

CONCLUSION: Don't Leave Home Without This Final Tip!.............139

ABOUT THE AUTHOR: Pat Williams...................................147

ABOUT THE WRITER: Peggy Matthews Rose....................149

ACKNOWLEDGMENTS...150

A Special Message of Tribute

> Pat Williams has written a comprehensive guide to winning a job interview. He takes into account all the complexities of a job search and makes the process clear, which is a valuable tool in today's marketplace. *Nail It!* is helpful, insightful—and well done.
>
> —DONALD J. TRUMP

I can't think of anyone who knows more about hiring and firing than the great Donald Trump. A business magnate and author, mega-successful real estate developer, in-demand face of real estate for other developers, Chairman and CEO of the Trump Organization, founder of Trump Entertainment Resorts, and so much more, this brilliant businessman is unrivaled in understanding what it takes to succeed in today's job market. He is truly a one-man conglomerate. In the face of devastating losses in the late 1980s and early 1990s, Donald Trump rebuilt his empire and has delivered it to unequaled heights, with complexes including two Trump Towers in New York City and the casinos Trump Taj Mahal, Trump Plaza, and Trump Marina. With a heart for equipping the next generation, he has authored at least fourteen books, with titles like Trump: The Art of the Deal *(1987),* Trump: The Art of the Comeback *(1997), and the recent* Trump Never Give Up: How I Turned My Biggest Challenges into Successes *(2008). Beyond landing the right job, if succeeding in business is your heart's desire you'd do well to read one or more of Donald Trump's books—as soon as you've finished this one, of course.*

—PW

INTRODUCTION:

Why You Need to Read This Book—*Right Now!*

You need a job, and you need one now. For that reason alone—you need this book! As an NBA general manager and now senior vice president with more than four decades in the game, hiring and firing have been parts of my job description for a long time. I can zero in on a winner quicker than you can say "Simon Cowell." And I know you are a winner. All you need are a few pointers on how to play the game. That's what this book is all about.

In today's painfully tight job market, you already know that you are competing with millions of other job seekers. Whether you're a young person with your freshly printed college degree in hand or a newly minted senior citizen—laid off but not ready yet to retire—what can you do to compete and win in this no-margin marketplace?

Anyone who's ever been part of an "elimination round" process understands that the final decision usually rests upon a few key factors. What made that person stand out? What is it that gave them the edge, that "something extra"?

No question, today's job market is not unlike an *American Idol* audition—it's *that* competitive. So how do you win the job interview? I won't kid you—it's not easy. There are plenty of books on interviewing techniques and how to do job searches, but how can you know what a successful job candidate looks like—before you go in for the interview? And what can you do to make sure the reflection looks just like you?

Several years ago, when the Orlando Magic were interviewing for a key executive position, a committee was formed to screen applicants. My assistant at that time, Marlin Busher, headed the committee. After sifting through dozens of applications, the group finally narrowed it down to ten people. They conducted in-person interviews with all ten and began the thankless task of eliminating various candidates.

When the dust had settled, there were two contenders left standing.

I said to Marlin, "What did these two have that the others didn't? What did you see that has allowed them to stay alive in the process?" Marlin shared with me the qualities the committee had seen that let these two rise like cream to the top of the crop.

Little did I know that this conversation with Marlin would launch me on what has become a ten-year research project— one that I'm still conducting to this day. What is it that makes a job applicant shine? How can we make sure we're ready when that magic moment comes? What is that *certain something* each of us needs to grasp if we hope to take hold of the brass ring on the next go-round of this carousel called life?

I've spent my entire life in the sports world and I can say with confidence that nowhere is it tougher to succeed. It's my hope that the insight I share with you in this book will give you a leg up in building your own life résumé.

There are ten qualities Marlin outlined and, after talking with many human resources executives, I am convinced these qualities are universal. Over these next several pages, my goal is to help you cut through the confusion to these universal ten top qualities for making every job search a successful one. Together, let's create a successful job candidate who looks just like you.

CHAPTER 1:

Network

When do you know it's time to eat? Do you wait until your stomach sounds like a jungle cat on the prowl, or until your body is so emaciated the anatomy professor mistakes you for the teaching skeleton? Of course not. You may eat because it's your designated mealtime, or you may eat simply because you're hungry—or because the guy two cubicles over yelled out, "Pizza!" Your body comes equipped with a mechanism that lets you know when you need sustenance. If you need to go make a sandwich right now, go right ahead. I'll wait.

Similarly, we discover we need the company of others when we experience a feeling called loneliness, or encounter a situation in which we feel helpless. We are wired to need other people. I have learned that the more people you know, the happier and more successful your life is likely to be.

Isn't it enough, you might ask, to have a family who loves you and a handful of close amigos? Maybe a few dozen "friends" on Facebook? Well, yes . . . and no.

Our families comprise the most important people in our lives—no question. I am blessed beyond measure to have my beloved wife, Ruth, in my life. And then there are our nineteen amazing children (yes, nineteen; did I mention I love big families?), and our eight—so far—grandchildren. No one fills up my life more than these wonderful people and I simply can't get enough of their company.

When it comes to friends, we can count ourselves fortunate to have even a handful of people we can trust, those partners we can go to when life hurts or when we need to sort out a big decision. I'm a big believer in small groups—a close circle of friends who get together on a regular basis to discuss life topics and who generally "do life together." If you don't have a group of friends like this, I strongly urge you to find one!

Loneliness is the most terrible poverty.

– MOTHER TERESA

But beyond the family and close friends, we need a network—a database of people to whom we can turn when the time comes—because we never know when that time will come. Beyond those favored few we call family and friends, we need that phone book, that Outlook or Plaxo address file, that contact menu of people who can help us get where we need to go—whether we're making a career move, recruiting ballplayers, or planning an event. The thing is, you may not know at the moment who those people are. So my advice to you is to cast your net wide and be ready. I call it being a "people collector."

PEOPLE! WHO NEEDS 'EM?

We all have moments when we throw up our hands in amazement at the antics of others and mutter about having to put up with them. But really, what would we do without people?

Like it or not, you need people in your life. I need them. We all need each other. We men tend to think we can get by on our own. Many's the old western movie hero who would mutter through tightly set lips, "I don't need no one. I can do jest fine by myself!" It's not true.

In his book *The Pursuit of Wow!*, author Tom Peters observes that women hold the edge when it comes to networking. For them, gathering people is instinctive, probably because they have the brains and good sense to know they'll need someone else's advice at some point. We tough guys, on the other hand, tend to think of networking as "sissy stuff," Peters asserts. "But truth is, it has always been the age of 'networkers'; and in an era where organizations depend more and more on tenuously connected outsiders to get the job done, it will only become more so."[1]

I'm not trying to sound sexist here, but simply to acknowledge that men and women approach life differently. I don't think you'll argue with me on that. And when it comes to networking, you women have it wired. We all need to cultivate this skill.

Professionally, it's not really who you know. We've been taught that for years, haven't we? The truth is, it's who knows what you know. Who have you worked with or for? If you're new to the professional world, consider your professors or lab partners or counselors, even your classmates or co-workers at the jobs you held in college. Do whatever it takes to begin building a base of potential employers, employees, sub-contractors. The possibilities are endless. I know it can be tempting, when you leave a school or workplace, to want to leave it all behind and start fresh. Nothing wrong with that, but please remember that your former colleagues *are* your network. Do what it takes to stay connected professionally. By the way, that includes being careful not to burn any bridges. As much as it's up to you, leave on a positive note.

In today's world, establishing a network has become both essential *and* easier than ever. Becoming known to others for what you do well is critical. As an executive who is frequently in the position to hire, I can tell you that when I need someone to fill a job, the first place I'll start looking is in my contact list, my menu of people I've collected. Who do I already know who knows how to do this job? It happens in every industry and it's not about favoritism; it's just smart business practice. Why spend hours and days searching for someone when the perfect candidate is right at your fingertips already?

Attorney Robert Kerrigan has said, "The way of the world is meeting people through other people." I can't over-emphasize how true this is. Ever since my daughter Karyn moved to Nashville in 2007, I've been amazed to discover how many people know someone who lives in Nashville. I tell them, "Look up my daughter!" And do you know, sometimes they do. Ever since my kids were little I've taught them the importance of building relationships. It's been wonderful to see that networking magic go to work for Karyn, as every now and then she'll call to say she just had coffee with one of those folks.

The late great business guru Peter Drucker once observed, "More business decisions occur over lunch and dinner than at any other time, yet no MBA courses are given on the subject." I hope you'll think of this chapter as your mini-MBA course on networking.

It isn't just what you know, and it isn't just who you know. It's actually who you know, who knows you, and what you do for a living.

–BOB BURG, NETWORKING EXPERT

The current size of your network isn't important. What matters is that you grow it, like an investment portfolio. I remember reading the story of young John Culhane, who was delirious at being invited to visit the Walt Disney home by schoolmate Diane, Walt's oldest daughter. During an unexpected meeting with Walt himself, Disney gave the young writer-in-training some sage advice: start small, Walt told him, and then widen your circles.

Gail Brown of Exceeding Expectations, a company that specializes in training and motivational programs, told me, "Through networking you expand your sphere of influence. Everyone you know knows 250 people, and so on."

Toss a pebble in a pond and watch the effect it has on the water. Now think of yourself as that little pebble—ever increasing your ripple of influence.

ENDLESS OPPORTUNITIES

If you're changing careers in mid-stream or found yourself, as so many have, laid off after years with one company or profession, you've probably already begun building that contact file. If you haven't, please listen to me: I know it's tempting to feel sorry for yourself and cuddle up with your crying towel. Don't do it!

Just because one door has closed does not mean other doors aren't waiting for your push to open them. The most fruitful way to look at this moment of your life is to see it as a new adventure, an opportunity for new learning, for meeting new people.

Life is really all about relationships, after all. Do what you can to maintain those contacts with old friends and co-workers while knocking hard on every door before you, ready for the one that yields to your touch. Throw that crying towel in the corner where it belongs and get back in the game.

Or maybe you're a young person who's thinking—*OK, I should network. I get it! But how do I do it? After all, I've been in school my whole life, so how can I get to know people in the field I want to explore?*

From former NFL Head Coach, George Allen:

GAME PLAN AFTER LOSING A JOB

1. Be yourself.

2. Have no regrets.

3. Don't count on friends for help.

4. Get out of the house.

5. Work out physically, hard.

6. Do something you've always wanted to do.

7. Plant a seed, every day.

8. Ask for advice from someone you respect.

9. Help someone who needs it.

10. You'll be tempted to be negative—resist it! Be positive.

11. Do something to improve yourself, every day.

12. Be direct. Research and follow up on job leads yourself.

13. Keep fighting.

14. Keep reading.

There are so many ways, even I don't know them all. But let's explore just a few.

You can build a professional network among your friends, professors, family, church, neighbors, and community. Professional networks built through online groups are growing in popularity. When it comes right down to it, the only person who can limit your network reach is you.

All professional athletes know there is a time coming when they will need to find a new career path. Not even Kobe Bryant will be playing basketball professionally in his fifties. Rare is the person in this day and age who works at any one job or career his or her entire life. I've been blessed to be in professional sports all my working days, but even within that field I've changed roles and teams many times. And I can say unequivocally that every one of those upward moves came as the result of networking—of getting to know and be known by others. We *all* need each other!

I began my career in professional sports playing for the Phillies farm club in Miami, Florida. At the age of twenty-two, I bought a book by legendary baseball owner Bill Veeck that changed my life and led to a relationship I'll always treasure. Veeck was a colorful character, a man who had owned a string of baseball teams—the Cleveland Indians, the St. Louis Browns, and the Chicago White Sox. He was well known for the over-the-top antics he'd pull to bring people into the ballparks. So when I saw that book, *Veeck, as in Wreck*, about my baseball hero, I had to have it.

Social networking sites like Myspace, Friendster, and Facebook have literally exploded in popularity in just a few short years.

–MIKE FITZPATRICK, CONGRESSMAN[2]

In the first chapter, he made mention of a man who just happened to be the general manager of the team I was playing with for that season, Bill Durney. At season's end, I told Bill, "More than anything, I'd love to meet Bill Veeck." And do you know what? Bill Durney arranged for that to happen! That September of 1962 I made the drive from my home in Wilmington, Delaware to Veeck's home in Easton, Maryland and ended up spending five hours with this amazing man. Those five hours turned into a friendship and mentorship that lasted twenty-five years. And it started with a book!

Don't pass up any opportunity to meet people. You never know where just one relationship might lead.

Maybe you've led a sheltered life. You might be thinking, "I don't know anyone!" As unlikely as that may be, it's certainly possible that your contact pool is limited at the moment. But it doesn't have to stay that way.

Today's world has possibilities for networking that we hadn't even dreamed of back when I was starting my career. Just imagine if Bill Veeck had been on Twitter or Facebook. Even if you're shy, you can use these online resources. It all goes back to who you know who knows what you know. Of course, as with anything you do online, exercising caution is highly recommended.

Keep your eyes and ears out for job fairs in your area—either your geographical area or your career field. Most companies who participate send out their best human resources people, so it's not only a great way to get introduced to the company but it's a wonderful way to let your light shine in their direction as well.

We'll talk more about the job interview in our next chapter. That's a changing world, and we've got to be ready to take it on, head first, if we're going to nail that job.

COLLECTING PEOPLE

My favorite way to connect is to *simply talk to people.* The truth is that most of us find our next job by word-of-mouth. If it hasn't happened that way for you yet, I'll bet you know at least one other person for whom it has. Why not interview them and get their story? Finding out how other people got their break is a good way to make a few of your own—and yes, I did say "make." Breaks don't usually come our way while we wait for them. We've got to apply a little old-fashioned elbow grease.

Start with your family, your friends, people you know at church, former co-workers. Don't be shy! Wherever you go, whomever you might encounter—strike up a conversation. Ask things like, "So how do you like your job?" "How did you get into that field?" "Is this what you've always wanted to do?" You'll be surprised at how these simple questions—asked sincerely and with genuine interest in the answers—might open up doors for you personally.

It's all about people. It's about networking and being nice to people and not burning any bridges.

–MIKE DAVIDSON, DESIGNER

I've authored more than fifty books so far, and all of them have been written with the assistance of a wordsmith I met through networking. Without exception, I met the perfect writer for my book project through someone I knew, somewhere I went, or some other project I was working on. Learn to put all social moments to work for you. I'm not talking about making life a contest, but simply about making connections. The best ones I know are those that last a lifetime. They are the contacts who become your friends and who enrich your life in immeasurable ways.

One of my closest friends today is a man named Ken Hussar. Ken is not an athlete, former basketball manager, or anyone with whom I ever worked in professional sports. He is a former schoolteacher. We met over thirty years ago, back when I was general manager for the Philadelphia 76ers. I was speaking at an event one night and Ken was part of the evening's musical entertainment. When we had a few moments to speak to one another, it turned out our senses of humor were bent in the same direction. So we hit it off and began collecting jokes.

That friendship has led so far to three books on humor and Ken has been part of almost everything I've worked on. Today, I can count on Ken to proofread every manuscript I write with courtesy and professionalism. We continue to make one another laugh today.

Like my friend Ken, your best contacts may not always be people with whom you work on a regular basis, or even people who work in your career path. I've seen way too many people close themselves off into a tight inner circle of only those who share their common interests. Don't do that to yourself! You never know where a great friendship may be waiting to find you.

At the beginning of this chapter I talked about the power of having a small group of friends. Call it a club or a circle of friends or the gang you hang with at the coffee shop or whatever label you want to slap on it, but I'm talking about a group of people with whom you meet regularly for discussion and support—people who feed into one another's lives in positive, affirming ways. I really can't over-emphasize the power of these connections. Today more than ever, we need each other. Did you know that the Bible uses the phrase "one another" more than almost any other? We are made for community. No matter how tough and self-reliant you think you are, you need others in your life. I know I do, and you do too. Networking is a key that unlocks the door to success.

Becoming a more human leader involves confessing one's need for others.

–DAN ALLENDER, AUTHOR, *Leading with a Limp*

Before we close this chapter, I want to make one thing clear. Networking is *not* about using people. It's easy to think that it is, given so many of the images we've seen in movies or TV and heard about over the years. But it's not true, not at all. Networking is about valuing others. It's about recognizing we are on this planet and in this time together for a reason—to help one another. It's what we are made for. When you discover that truth—and not until you discover that truth—your worldview will come into focus like never before. Think about how differently so many of the headlines just in this past year might have read had the players involved only learned that lesson in advance. Stories involving character assassination, failed marriages and partnerships, fraud and political posturing would go way down, if we just saw our lives and our roles in that light, the perspective that says, "How can I help you?" I strongly urge you to learn it now! Living as the Lone Ranger will only get you misfired silver bullets.

YOUR JOB INTERVIEW NAIL GUN: NETWORKING

1. Keep a business card file.

2. Use a tool to keep track of people who can help you go to that next level in life. I use a Franklin Planner, but there are many others: your computer address book, your smart phone, a Day-Timer, or even an old-fashioned phone book.

3. Take advantage of online tools for professionals, like Monster.com, Ladders, LinkedIn, and other sites created especially to help you connect with others in the workplace and find sources of jobs.

4. Go to seminars and workshops whenever you can—and get to know the folks in your row. I heard a great new term the other day that describes using your free time for getting work done, so let me use it here—make sure you're making productive use of your "weisure" time!

5. Be on the lookout for job fairs in your area, and whatever you do—don't find an excuse to stay home.

6. Make people-collecting a way of life. You won't regret it.

CHAPTER 2:

Be Interview Question-Ready

American humorist Jack Handey once wrote, "When you go in for a job interview, I think a good thing to ask is if they ever press charges."[3] He was joking, of course, but if you don't want your interview to be arrested before it's over, you've got to be ready for any type of question.

Know your strengths and areas for development. Be able to describe your short- and long-term goals and then relate them to the position you are applying for. What job do you want? Be able to describe how you would approach the first thirty, sixty, and ninety days in the position if selected. Know how your ideas fit with the company's vision.

Be able to answer, "Where do you see yourself in five years? Ten years?" Prospective employers are interested in knowing how driven you are to succeed and grow professionally.

What we're really talking about here is having a life plan. When you have some idea of where you're going, it's a whole lot easier to chart a course to take you there. Our problem is, over time we naturally tend to become complacent and drift off course. So it's critical that we, like skilled airline pilots, chart our headings and monitor the instruments regularly to keep our lives from crashing.

As a first step in being interview-question ready, why not start by figuring out where it is you want to end up in your career life? Think of it as a roadmap.

Have a plan in your life and be able to adjust it. Have a plan, when you wake up, what you're going to do with your day. Just don't go lollygagging through any day of your life.

– PAUL W. "BEAR" BRYANT, LEGENDARY
COLLEGE FOOTBALL COACH

YOUR LIFE ROAD MAP

Some folks say life is random, but I don't believe that for a minute. I believe each one of us is here for a reason and that we're created to do something only we can do. Accept your life's intentionality and I believe you'll be quantum leaps closer to plotting that map. So what can you do to discover your personal sweet spot? How can you know what it is you are meant to do?

People have been asking the question, "Why was I born?" since time itself began. Fortunately for you and me, a few of them have written books on their personal journeys. There's plenty of advice out there for those of you who want to discover the meaning of life or cut a new swath for yourself—books like *Escape from Cubicle Nation: From Corporate Prisoner to Thriving*

Entrepreneur, by Pamela Slim (Portfolio Hardcover, 2009), or the practical *How to Find the Perfect Job in 30 Days or Less,* by Paul Fontaine (iUniverse, 2002).

Other books like *Only You Can Be You,* by Erik Rees (Howard Books, 2009) help you figure out what you are meant to do with your life based on five major components: our gifts, what we're most passionate about, our abilities, our personalities, and our experiences. Books like this one make great life roadmap tools.

Our gifts are the tools we use in helping people, like encouragement, hospitality, or teaching. Where do others find help or comfort from you? Write down what you see.

What do you love to do? I've always held that if you can find a way to do what it is you love, you'll never work a day in your life. In other words, if what you're doing is what you love to do, it won't seem like work at all. Do you know what that one thing is? Write it down.

What abilities do you have? Are you a natural singer, writer, athlete, or craftsperson? Where did you earn the As and Bs in school? You fill in the blank. Where do you need to buff and polish those abilities? If you were a product, what would make someone say, "I gotta have that"? These answers require brutal honesty. But I have faith in you—you can do this! Remember, you are the CEO of Yourself.com.

Now let's talk about your persona. No matter what others tell you—you are who you are for a reason! What do your natural traits tell you about the kind of work you might be happiest doing?

Next are your life's experiences. Maybe you are coming out of a long-held job and trying to figure out what's next. Even the most carefully charted roadmaps often change course, after all. That's just being realistic. So here's where you lean a little on the past in order to figure out your future.

My writing partner in this book, for example, came out of a long career with the Disney Company, wondering what was next for her. She knew her abilities, and when it came to experience, she'd spent years studying the life of Walt Disney. As networking magic would have it, she attended an annual book event in her community at which I was a featured author.

Neither of us had any idea that a partnership was about to be born, as she stood in line to get a book signed and talk to me about *Go for the Magic!* (Nelsonword Publishing Group, 1995), a book I'd written a few years earlier on the business principles of Walt Disney. How could she have known that, at that very moment, I was working on *How to Be Like Walt Disney* (HCI, 2004)? And how could I have known she would be such a rich resource of contacts and information about this amazing man? Jim Denney, my partner on that book, and I agree the final result would have been much thinner without her help.

My point in sharing this anecdote is that you never know when or where those pivotal life moments are going to occur unless you are open to new opportunities and ready for them to reveal themselves when you least expect them.

What's in your personal arsenal of experiences that might qualify you in a unique way to help someone else? No one else has lived the life you have lived or done exactly the things you have done. Go out and apply the lessons life has taught you.

One leader I know encourages his staff to map out a pencil plan each year. The word "pencil" implies room left for changing what needs remapping along the way. That's a great idea! Why not develop a pencil plan of your own?

And that brings up two more points:

1) I've often heard it said that if you want to make God laugh, tell him your plans. The reality is this: life is not a trip to the grocery store, New York, or even the moon. No matter where we may want to go, few of us end up where we thought we were going when we started. So while the roadmap we're discussing here is a great planning tool, we need to accept the fact that things are going to happen that will change those plans.

A few years ago, I wrote a book called *The Three Success Secrets of Shamgar* (Faith Communications, 2004), about a character in the biblical book of Judges. The secrets are to start where you are, use what you have, and do what you can. Even without reading the book, you can tell where it is going just by looking at those principles. There is no guaranteeing our destination in life, but when you start where you are, use what you have, and do what you can—the potential for where you can go is limitless.

2) We've got to keep in mind that message from chapter one: that we are here to help the others around us. If we go into our job search thinking only of helping ourselves, we really can't hope to get very far. It's only when we turn ourselves inside out and begin asking others the question, "How can I help you?" that we begin to discover who we really are. Life is often ironic that way.

One other thing: when you're making that life plan, don't be afraid to dream big. The poet Robert Browning once wrote, "Ah, but a man's reach should exceed his grasp—or what's a heaven for?" This world still needs big dreamers. I'm convinced there are amazing things yet to be accomplished, so go ahead and grab as much of that blue sky as you can.

The person who makes a success of living is the one who sees his goal, steadily, and aims for it, unswervingly. That is dedication.

– CECIL B. DEMILLE

One of the great advantages we have here in the 21st century is a plethora of tools. When I was a young man, such help was largely non-existent. You might occasionally find a book on interview preparation, but nothing like the many seminars and books available today. So I followed my heart.

I grew up surrounded by sports, as many boys do. When I was seven years old, my dad gave me Pop Warner's *Book for Boys*, and I'd have to say that this book became the compass for my life. Glenn "Pop" Warner taught me everything I needed to know about teamwork, sportsmanship, winning, leadership, and more. These lessons were foundational for me. Of course, as a young man I'd envisioned myself playing big league baseball one day. That didn't happen. Oh, I made it to the Phillies farm club, but that's as close as I got. It turned out my gifts for helping others as well as my abilities fit me far better for a position in the front office. And while in time I "bounced" from baseball to basketball, it's a career choice I'm so glad I made. I wouldn't trade my Magic life for anything.

All this is to say that the course of our roadmap is often determined by influences in our young lives—those experiences we mentioned a few paragraphs ago. In fact, I'd hazard to say that this is true more often than not.

What got your attention most when you were a kid in school? Is there a way to recapture that youthful enthusiasm and channel it into a career path? Believe it or not, even negative experiences can have a positive purpose, if we're willing to look at them in that way. Is there something haunting your life, a bad memory of a deep hurt? You are not the only one who has suffered. Perhaps your experience, coupled with your survivor attitude, can help someone else through a similar trial.

Only you can answer the questions we've raised here, but once you do you'll have taken the first steps to being interview-question ready. You'll know where you see yourself in five years, or ten, and what you ultimately hope to accomplish with your life. You'll know what you have to contribute. And what's more, you'll be motivated, because you'll see that job as another stepping-stone on the pathway of your life. That kind of vision, by the way, also helps you accept any failures in life—but we'll talk about that a little later on.

A big part of getting our act together is getting a vision for our lives. But the closest most people get to goal setting is making a list of New Year's resolutions, which last only a short time. Goals are so much more. They are dreams . . . with a deadline.

– STEPHEN STRANG, PUBLISHER

BUT, DUDE, I JUST NEED A JOB!

As important as it is to have dreams, it's true enough that sometimes we just need to find work—whether it's a career move or not. When the money from our last regular 'gig' is stretched too thin by our bills, almost anything will do. But even if it's not your dream job, you still need to be ready for that interview. It's going to matter a lot how you answer those key questions.

Study the job description and then hone in on where your experience best matches what the employer is looking for. Send a résumé in advance, topped by a cover letter that highlights your key qualifications, as outlined by the job description itself. Focus on what you can bring to the employer's table rather than on how desperate you are for the job. If you were the interviewer, what would make you want to take a second look?

No matter what job you're interviewing for, you're likely to be asked questions that cover two categories: your life direction—covered by that roadmap—and your behavior. How are you likely to act in a certain situation?

Be ready with positive stories about how you solved a crisis or made a decision that saved the day. Now I'm not talking about making up a story! Don't get me wrong. You've got to go after this job honestly or no one will win in the end. But think about the job description. What kinds of decisions might you need to make if you were to win this role? When were you in a similar situation and what did you do? Even a wrong past decision can be a positive example if you show that you've learned from it.

YOUR JOB INTERVIEW NAIL GUN: BE INTERVIEW-QUESTION READY

1. Take candid stock of your life and write out your own roadmap for where you hope to go. Be sure to use a pencil.

2. Know your own strengths and weaknesses—then focus on the strengths. Consider a class or program to develop what's lacking as you continue to build your strengths.

3. Research and review potential job interview questions to help plan your (honest) answers. This is not about rehearsing—it's about being prepared.

4. Even if what you find is "just a job," consider how that job can build you into a better person, as well as what you can uniquely contribute.

5. Practice! Practice! Practice!

CHAPTER 3

Be Prepared

By 1907, Lord Baden-Powell, renowned hero of the British Boer War, had decided to turn his attention to a more peaceful occupation—that of teaching young boys how to be ready for whatever physical trials life might bring their way. That year, the boys held their first meeting around a campfire in Dorsetshire, England, and by 1908, Baden-Powell published *Scouting for Boys*. The Boy Scouts were born. "Success was immediate and far-reaching," wrote Sir Winston Churchill. "The simple uniform, khaki shorts and a shirt—within the range of the poorest—was founded upon that of General Baden-Powell's old corps, the South African Constabulary. The hat was the famous hat with the flat brim and pinched top which he had worn at Mafeking. The motto 'Be Prepared' was founded on his initials."[4]

Over the last 100 years since, Baden-Powell's idea has benefitted the lives of literally millions of boys and girls the world over (he also founded the Girl Guides, which inspired the Girl Scouts, formed by Juliette Gordon Low in 1912) with its simple, basic principle. It's one that has stood the test of time and it fits our purpose in this chapter: be prepared.

Preparation is essential for anything you set out to do. The great Olympic champion Jackie Joyner-Kersee observed, "It's better to look ahead and prepare than look back and regret." I've done enough of both to agree completely with this sentiment.

Like having that life roadmap, we've got to be fully prepared for what we hope to accomplish every day. Without a sense of urgency and the determination to get something done, we are apt to drift through life and find ourselves wondering where that life drifted off to. As Jack Nicholson's character observed in *The Bucket List*, all our days will seem "like smoke through a keyhole." Don't let that happen to you.

PREPARATION IS A LIFE ATTITUDE

Being prepared is about more than just getting ready for an event. I believe we must live with a mind-set of preparation.

Professional athletes live in a state of readiness. Our Magic players, like all NBA pros, spend a lot of time getting prepared for the game. They have a shooting session in the morning, eat a team meal together, come early to get in more practice, sit through a strategy session, visit the trainer to get their ankles taped, consult with assistant coaches, and a million other details. They know it's so important to be, as Norma Desmond was for Mr. DeMille, ready for your close-up.

But long before that moment for the action call has arrived, we must be preparing. It's critical to be ready for anything. I love what the great coach John Wooden has to say about this: "Failing to prepare is preparing to fail."

As a young boy I knew I wanted to spend my life in the world of professional sports. So I prepared by reading books on sports, watching every game I could take in, playing in all kinds of sports, getting to know, thanks to my dad and through family friends, adults who had been in the sports world and could give me pointers or introduce me to people who could help me get where I wanted to go. It was all preparation.

At the age of twenty-seven, I became a Christian and my life found an anchor. From that day forward, I began investing time every day in getting to know the God of the Bible. This habit prepares me not only for eternity, but also to be able to help others at a moment's notice. I believe the Bible is the greatest resource of wisdom ever written. Its words have guided me through many of life's storms.

Daily, I prepare my heart by spending time in God's Word. A habit of memorizing Scripture gives me truth for each day and keeps my mind agile—a great preparation for old age. You see, part of my life plan is to live a long, healthy life that includes being useful to others every day I draw breath— another goal that requires preparation.

My training plan includes eating good, nutritious food, drinking lots of pure water, and daily exercise. In my fifties, I became a marathon runner. Now, you may think that's an odd time of life to begin such an arduous endeavor, but it keeps me going! I tell my kids it's how I practice not quitting. If you want to live a long and useful life too, you might want to consider a few of these same foundational choices.

Before everything else, getting ready is the secret of success.

–HENRY FORD, AUTOMOBILE PIONEER

It's important to realize, no matter how many years you think you have in front of you, that life is oh so short. Why waste time? Hall of Fame quarterback Steve Young observed of his colleague, the great Jerry Rice, "The difference between Jerry Rice and everybody else is that one day he woke up and said, 'I'm going to be the greatest receiver of all time. I'm going to run and prepare.' While everyone else was watching Oprah or hanging out, he was making sure he was running instead of playing."[5]

I'm not saying we should cut out all goofing around. Relaxing definitely has a place and time in our lives. But why burn away the precious hours of your one and only life with activities that don't take you to the next level of your life plan? Preparation, the mindset of "I'm going to run and prepare," is a daily essential both for winning your job interview and for winning at life.

So how can you use this out-of-work time to prepare yourself for what's next? Is there a seminar you can attend, a mission trip you can take, a book you should read? Maybe it's time to go back to school and earn that MBA or PhD. While you're waiting for the next "You're hired!"—use your time wisely.

PREPARATION IS A DAILY NECESSITY

Before your body can get out of bed in the morning, your mind has to prepare it for action. Have you ever noticed that? It's so integrated and subtle you might not realize it, but your mind has to tell your body to move, to slide those legs over the edge of the bed, plop those doggies on the floor, convince your knees to straighten, and stand up. Think about that the next time you get up from your chair and notice the almost invisible process that must occur to simply move. Without some level of preparation, it could not happen.

Every day, we need to have a plan in mind for that next twenty-four hours. Maybe you worked at the same company or job for years, and every day it was, "same place, same thing." And now you are reeling a little from being laid off—but don't let this setback stop you from having a productive plan for every single day. That terrifying tap on the shoulder just might have been a wake-up call for you to re-engage in the game of life. Whatever you do, get out of bed and *do something*, every day.

Spur of the moment activities are wonderful when our lives have the margin to allow them—but the prepared life is ready to accomplish something, no matter what each day might bring.

I am a checklist kind of guy, so I fully relate to this concept of listing your goals. Nothing gives me greater satisfaction than checking off another "to do" on my list. Now maybe that idea sends you running away in tears. That's okay! I hear some people are like that. But find some way to track daily goals, because when it comes to getting that next job, the person who's primed and ready to go is likely to be the winner.

Start by setting modest goals that are meaningful, but attainable. For example, every Sunday night, write down four things that you want to accomplish for the following week; then, make sure that seven days later, when you make your next list, all four items have been crossed off.

–ARTHUR ASHE, TENNIS CHAMPION

PREPARATION IS HAVING A GAME PLAN

Know what kinds of jobs you're interested in pursuing and where those jobs are. One former headhunter who'd been successful at finding qualified candidates became frustrated when the candidates would fail to get the job. So he turned his scouting talent into a business in which he began advising clients on how to interview and land the job. When he did that, Nick Corcodillo "helped improve their success ratio by teaching them to pursue fewer companies, make the right contacts and deliver what companies are looking for in an interview."[6] Another word for this might be specialization, and I highly recommend it.

In reinventing the job search process, Corcodillo developed some unique principles for successful job hunting:

1. Instead of letting your résumé outline your history, let it sell the company on what you can do for them. Make it your professional sales piece, showing what you can do for them tomorrow, rather than a rehash of all your yesterdays. Lorisse Garcia, the Orlando Magic's manager of recruiting and organizational development, told me the résumé, if poorly prepared, can actually keep you from even getting the interview. We'll expand on that in just a bit.

2. When possible, apply directly to the person who'll do the hiring. This keeps you from becoming lost in a stack of papers in HR.

3. If you've been contacted by a headhunter, realize that the matchmaking has already happened. You've won a spot on the Dating Game, if you want it. It's your job now to find out if the company is right for you. Research it, find out something about its culture, its goals, and its competitors. You can do that through the Internet, but a better way is through talking with people who work there. One creative individual did this by looking for articles written by company employees, then would call them and ask to talk. In most cases, he would either get the interview or find out the company wasn't for him.

4. Keep in mind that the employer wants to hire you—that's why you're there.

5. Treat the interview as if it's your first day on the job. Adopting this attitude helps keep the interview from turning into a dull question/answer session and lets the real you shine through.

6. Once you get an offer, it's your turn to interview the company. Ask to meet the people you'll work with and see what kinds of tools you'll have at your disposal. By now, the company has decided it wants to hire you. It's your call at this point whether or not you want to hire that company.[7]

THE ALL-IMPORTANT RÉSUMÉ

In the popular musical *A Chorus Line*, one of the principle songs begins with the plaintive refrain, "Who am I, anyway? Am I my résumé?" Of course, you are so much more than that—but when it comes to getting a job, when it comes to getting your foot in the interviewer's door—the answer is, "Yes! You *are* your résumé."

So let's scoot our chairs up closer for a moment and take a good look at that résumé. When it comes to preparation, there is probably no single tool more critical to your success.

"People are just not getting that part," Lorisse said. "They're not spending enough time and energy on it, and all too often that keeps them from even getting the interview." It's not uncommon for her to recommend a candidate based on a great phone interview, only to have the hiring manager say, "But this résumé looks so flat. I don't see what they've got to offer." People often interview so much better than their résumé makes them look, Lorisse told me. So what can you do with that sales piece, your résumé, to improve your odds?

"Right now, the candidate pool is wide and deep—and people don't know how to write a résumé. As a recruiter, I have one job and maybe 300 candidates to review—so if you don't get your résumé right, you're not even going to get the interview." Lorisse stresses making your résumé preparation the key element in your job search. Remember: your résumé is your personal sales piece. What would make an employer want to buy into you?

There are so many services you can use, many of them free, to help you develop your résumé—there's really no excuse for a poor one. If you're a recent college graduate, tap into the alumni services at your school. Or use one of the many online services from companies like Career Builder, or

Monster, or Ladders. Of course, there are always independent professional services out there, too, to help you. Many large churches also offer career resources and often have networks made up from within their own membership to help each other with every piece of the job search.

Speaking of churches, another move Lorisse recommends is using your time between jobs to build that résumé through volunteering. What a great idea! Show your community spirit by getting involved helping people in an area of interest for you. What do you know you could teach or where do you have a heart to help others? One pastor I know recommends volunteering as a way to hone your career search, and it certainly allows you to use and develop your passions in ways the job market itself can often stifle. So go for it! Not only will volunteerism develop you personally while it helps someone else, but it tells the interviewer you're not someone who sits around waiting for your next gig. Volunteering is a win-win.

And then be creative in crafting that résumé. Be willing to do extra work to tailor it for the specific job or industry you're after. "I've been in HR for over twenty-six years," Lorisse recalled, "and the most creative résumé I ever received, hands down, came just a couple of years back. In addition to a traditional copy of his résumé, this young man Fed-Exed to us a Gatorade bottle with his résumé as the label!" In place of the product name was the applicant's name, his background and strengths as the ingredients, and so on. "I'd stopped interviewing for this position, which was a web services manager, but his résumé was so clever and attention-grabbing, I had to give him a chance." He got the job, and though he has since left the organization, Lorisse keeps that Gatorade bottle to remind her how ingenuity so often wins the day. What kind of Gatorade bottle can you come up with? What would say, "I'm right for this job" in your chosen industry?

Finally, make sure you have someone who knows what they're doing review your résumé. Find a friend who's an English major or someone you know who works in human resources. Have them read your résumé and be willing to listen to their suggestions. Do "test run" phone interviews with friends or associates who can give you honest feedback. All of these suggestions can only help you.

Just as we were going to press with this book, the Magic office received another eye-popping example. Surprised by the delivery of a Papa John's pizza one July day, our HR representative was further stunned to discover a résumé and mock *Orlando Sentinel* news article attached inside the box, keeping the pepperoni company. Sent by a young man in Massachusetts, you know he'd gone to some work to make this extremely creative introduction. Will he get the job? That story is yet to be told. Qualifications, after all, are the final determinant. But he certainly had our attention.

HOW TO LIVE AND LOOK PREPARED

Let preparation be a mindset, an attitude, a lifestyle. I've often said that in the dating game, once you meet Mr. or Ms. Right, you're not likely to lose those fifty pounds in the next few minutes. I think you get my drift here. Be working on those things that need improvement all the time. If you do, then when the time comes, you'll be ready to meet it.

1. Find a mentor. Former UCLA basketball player Pete Blackman told me about a lesson he learned from legendary Coach John Wooden: "I learned from his extraordinarily detailed organization. He was fantastically prepared; literally every practice we planned down to the minute. You don't lose track of lessons like that. When you are preparing for a major business presentation fifteen years later, you look around and you're probably the best-prepared person there. Why is that true? Because people like Coach Wooden proved to you at an early stage of development, that the time spent in preparation will pay off." Mentors are a huge factor in living the prepared life. Who could be your Coach Wooden?

2. Have a purpose. Today, it might be finding a job, hopefully getting the one you're interviewing for. But you've got to think beyond today, beyond this job or even the next one. What exactly is it that you are living for?

3. Stay Relevant. Nothing hurts your chances for finding that next career move more than being forgotten. The old expression, "out of sight, out of mind" is true. When you left your last job you undoubtedly heard many times over as you said your goodbyes, "Let's keep in touch!" And those left-behind coworkers meant it. So how are you going to stay in touch? Email has made that relatively easy, as have some of those social and professional networking sites we mentioned earlier in this book. Be sure you do it.

Do whatever you can to keep your name out there. If you're a professional, are there magazine articles you can write on your craft, or maybe even a book? Or if that sounds too ambitious, how about a blog or even an occasional letter to the editor? We always think we can't go on without our best friend or favorite co-worker. But sadly, it only takes a few days to find out that we can. Don't let yourself become forgotten! How you accomplish that is up to you.

You never want to be a former anything.
People forget you real quick.

–DAVID JEREMIAH, PASTOR AND AUTHOR

---

4. Realize that preparation is the cure for worry.
Astronaut John Glenn is credited as saying, "The greatest antidote to worry, whether you're getting ready for space flight or facing a problem of daily life, is preparation. The more you try to envision what might happen and what your best response and options are, the more you are able to calm your fears about the future."

He is so right! Imagine yourself in the interview. What will they ask? How will you answer? What will you say if you don't know what to say? There are plenty of resources available to help you plan for a job interview. Check them out! There are books, websites, seminars—all kinds of tools. As much as you are able, put them to work for you.

Author and leadership expert John Maxwell challenges us to consider: "What happens when you don't prepare? Things you hoped won't happen do happen…and they occur with greater frequency than the things you hoped would happen. The reason is simple: being unprepared puts you out of position. Ask negotiators what happens at the bargaining table when they are out of position. They lose. Preparation positions people correctly, and it is often the separation between winning and losing."[8]

You've undoubtedly heard that famous prediction from our old friend Murphy, who said, "Anything that can go wrong will go wrong." We can pretty much count on it. So why not prepare for it?

Unanticipated moments are waiting for us everywhere, but preparation helps us be ready when they come. By researching the company, gathering information on potential interview questions, getting to know the job requirements for the position you're after, you are preparing yourself for almost anything. Consider all options; don't obsess. The "readier" you are when the moment comes, the more your natural brilliance will shine at just the right time.

THE BIG DAY IS HERE!

Some of the following tips may seen obvious, but I've seen people lose their way by neglecting these basics:

1. Do your homework: Know something about the company with which you are interviewing. Understand who they are and what their mission statement is. In most cases that information is plentifully available on the Internet. If possible, brush up on what's required of the position you're seeking. This shows initiative and professionalism.

You'd be surprised how many people show up for interviews just hungry for a job. I know it can be tempting to answer almost any ad when you've been out of work awhile, but it really is critical to know something about the company before you to talk to them. It shows the interviewer you care about the job.

In the world of professional sports, each team has its own culture and attitude, its own unique DNA. Each team has its own personality. The same is true in the business world. So even if you left one aircraft manufacturer to work for another, don't assume you're working with the same people—because you're not!

John Wooden's teams had great talent, but they had great character too. They were so well-prepared that he didn't even coach very much during the games. They knew how to play and they went out and played.

– BILL BRADLEY, FORMER U.S. SENATOR AND
FORMER HALL OF FAME BASKETBALL PLAYER

---

2. Know how to get there. If you've ever gotten lost trying to get to an unfamiliar location, you already know what you did wrong. If your interview is in a part of town you've never been to, make sure you know the location and do a dry run on directions. Consider the time of day in which you'll be driving and the potential traffic situations at that time. Take a book with you so that if you arrive too early, you can go somewhere to enrich your mind while you wait, or go over your interview answers one more time. The idea is to be on time, ready for the interview, and, as much as possible, not overly nervous.

3. Have a résumé with you. Have extra copies of your résumé with you, as well as your professional references. Bring copies of your best work—copies you can leave with the interviewer.

Being prepared, like being interview-question ready, involves taking stock of your life. Where have you been? Where do you hope to go? What is the best way to get there?

In the summer of 1968, I was in my fourth year with the Spartanburg Phillies, fully believing that professional baseball was my life. One day I found a note on my desk to return a call from Jack Ramsay, who was then general manager of the Philadelphia 76ers. Would I be interested, he asked, in becoming the 76ers business manager, running the day-to-day front office?

At twenty-eight years old, I was totally geared to a life in baseball—but I knew opportunity when I saw it. I flew up to meet Ramsay. We had a wonderful interview and he offered me a job for three years at $20,000 a year—a fortune in those days to a young man like me. I flew back elated.

Two days later, Jack called. "We've got a problem," he said, and my heart sank. "The owner of the team is not comfortable with this hiring and wants you to come back up." Within moments I'd gone from elation over my new job to analyzing the situation. Was it the right move for me?

When I got to Philadelphia, I was told to report to Dr. Norman Gekoski. I had no idea I was about to meet with a psychologist! It turned out the 76ers' owner, Irv Kosloff, used him to help screen potential employees. So I went through a whole morning of psychological testing.

Dr. Gekoski then put me in a cab and sent me to meet with Kosloff's banker. From there I was sent to Kosloff's accountant and then to his lawyer. After that, I met with Eddie Gottleib, Kosloff's basketball guru.

By now it was 6 p.m. and my head was spinning. Irv and Mrs. Kosloff met me and took me to dinner. Just before I got on the plane back to Spartanburg, Mr. Kosloff said, "I want to hire you."

That's how I joined the NBA, forty-one years ago.

The message I want you to hear in my story is this: be ready for anything. If you want the job, you've got to respond to the potential employer's request. Keep your cool—and have plenty of money for cab fare!

YOUR JOB INTERVIEW NAIL GUN: BE PREPARED

1. Whether you are working right now or not, have a plan for every single day. Develop a checklist and mark it off—it's a practice that pays off with a tremendous sense of accomplishment.

2. Develop an attitude of preparation. It's a life skill that will take you far.

3. Mentally prepare by imagining yourself in the interview: what could go wrong? Be ready for it.

4. Always have your résumé ready—and be sure it says, "I'm the one you want"!

5. When that interview call comes, be sure you know where you're going to go and map out your directions ahead of time.

6. Be on time.

JOB FAIR TIPS

With so many candidates squeezing in to job fairs these days, how can you make yourself stand out? In his article "How to Stop Fishing at Job Fairs," Brent Peterson of *Interview Angel* offers these sound tips:

1. If possible, check out the job fair's website in advance to find out who will be there.

2. Based on the list, determine whom you want to get to know and why and then research those companies.

3. Develop your résumé targeted for those companies you've decided you want to check out.

4. Even if there are no companies or positions open at the job fair for you, use the opportunity to network and build contacts. Peterson cautions that "you should treat it that way going in," however. Keep your expectations positive and realistic.

5. See the job fair as an opportunity to meet prospective employers and not as a job interview itself. Avoid handing out résumés to companies you haven't scouted or know nothing about. "Employer representatives are doing initial screenings," Peterson says, "and they can tell who has seriously researched them and who is fishing." The résumés from "fishermen" rarely get a second look.

6. Be sure to dress *professionally* and act exactly as you would if you were going to a job interview.

7. Arrive as early as possible.

8. Have on hand:

   □ A professional padfolio

   □ A working pen and notepad

   □ Copies of your résumé

   □ Business cards

9. Go directly to the tables of the companies you've pre-screened.

10. Introduce yourself and offer the elevator speech you've been practicing (we'll talk more about the elevator speech in Chapter 5).

11. Be ready to interview at the fair if the opportunity arises.

12. Be ready to schedule any appointments that may be arranged (know your own calendar).

13. Be sure you have silenced your cell phone.

14. Ask for business cards from those with whom you speak.

15. Follow up. As soon as possible, send thank you notes to anyone you may have spoken with at the fair.

16. Be professional and courteous at all times.

17. If you have not heard back from them after a week, it's appropriate to place a follow-up phone call.

CHAPTER 4:

Display Professionalism

E nter the words "what does it mean to be professional" into your Google search engine and you'll find that over four million web surfers want to know the answer to that question, too. So while on the surface it sounds like a no-brainer, this fourth universal quality is clearly not one that's easily grasped.

Many people think that to be a "professional" simply means you are being paid for the work you do, as opposed to an "amateur" who is not paid. They may even consider that the two words distinguish one's ability to do the work. Yet the word amateur comes from the Latin word "amator," or lover. So you could argue that a professional, then, engages in a pursuit for the money that's in it, while the amateur does what he does for the love of it. Which one would you rather hire?

Clearly, being a professional is about far more than just being paid. After all, if you do a poor job but are paid for it, you are hardly displaying professionalism.

Some people think that being "professional" applies to how you present yourself physically—how you dress, wear your hair, and generally carry yourself through the world. There is some truth to that idea. If we expect to win the job interview, not to mention winning at life, we've got to get our minds around what it means to be "professional." It begins with our personal appearance.

WHAT *NOT* TO WEAR

The story is told that when George Washington attended pre-Revolutionary War congressional meetings, he would appear in full military uniform. He was not yet the Commander in Chief of the American armed forces, but his choice of attire helped fix that notion in the minds of his compatriots. He wanted the part and looked the part—and when the time came, he got the part. George Washington knew how to dress for success.

Former President Washington understood "dressing for success" long before it became a business byword. When you are preparing yourself for that interview, be sure to dress appropriately for the job and the industry you seek.

In matters of style, swim with the current;
in matters of principle, stand like a rock.

– THOMAS JEFFERSON

In addition to how you look on paper, you'll be judged by how you look in person. That might not sound "fair," but we all do it, everyday.

I spend a lot of time in the public arena. In fact, I am *literally* in sports arenas several nights a week on the average. And let me tell you, what passes for fashion today is enough to make me pass out! Real style is classic in nature, and that is always your best bet when it comes to dressing professionally. Remember—dress for the job you want, not the one you have. This is sound, seasoned advice. So take it!

If your wardrobe is lacking or is unfashionable, maybe now is a good time to invest in updating your look. Not sure how? There are plenty of resources out there.

I had a very close relationship with the late Chuck Daly, longtime college and NBA coach. In fact, I hired him to his first coaching job with the Philadelphia 76ers. Chuck was not only an outstanding coach, he was the best-dressed coach in history, and he became a mentor to everyone else on how to dress.

After Chuck joined the 76ers, he took me under his wing. "Never pay retail," he told me, as he took me around to all the stores where the best deals could be found. He taught me how to match pants to shirts, shirts to ties, socks to trousers, and so much more. He took me to his barber in South Jersey with instructions on how to cut my hair. Nobody, but nobody, looked better than Chuck, and nobody he tutored will ever forget his lessons. He was the model of sartorial splendor.

So let me be your Chuck Daly for a moment. *Always* look good. *Always* dress well. It's too important for you not to make that choice. Take pride in your appearance. We've got a generation of young people out there who are not convinced you even need to *shave* everyday. I'm telling you to make that the first thing you do every morning. Gentlemen, you get up and you shave, before you do anything else. Then you get dressed and make sure you look as good as you possibly can before you set one foot out that door.

Clothes make the man. Naked people have little or no influence on society.

-MARK TWAIN

My wife Ruth's mother taught her years ago to never leave the house unless she was dressed at the highest level—the complete package had to be elegantly wrapped, or forget it. To this day, she won't even go down to the 7-Eleven store without full make-up, hair done, and looking very good. She might be dressed casually, but she's ready for anything. Even after all these years of running marathons together, she still carries a lipstick in her fanny pack. We know the Boston Marathon is almost over when she pulls her lipstick out around Boylston Street. The point is this: you never know who you're going to meet at the 7-Eleven, or Borders bookstore, or Starbucks, or anywhere you're out in the public eye. Always, always, always—look your best.

This is your job interview we're talking about here, so work hard at making everything look good. Whatever you do, find professional attire that's flattering to your body type and that fits. Nothing looks worse than showing up in a suit coat that fit twenty pounds ago. And ladies, please avoid those low-slung trousers some young women like that give them what I've heard aptly described as "muffin tops." That's exactly what it looks like, and believe me when I tell you, this look is *not* attractive. It might get you attention, but it will *not* get you the job you want. Trust me on that.

TIPS ON DRESSING FOR A JOB INTERVIEW

1. Be neat.

   - No wrinkles.

   - No stains.

   - Clothes not too short or too tight.

   - One bag or briefcase and nothing else. One human resources professional I spoke with suggested a small bag for the ladies. "You don't need the kitchen sink," she told me.

   - No gum.

   - No iPod or other distracting device. Turn your cell phone off.

   - No beverages.

   - Be sensible and conservative. If you happen to have a lot of tattoos or body piercings, this is not the time to advertise them.

2. No tennis shoes! Wear polished, conservative shoes.

3. Men: be sure to wear dark socks.

4. Hair that is neatly groomed and professionally styled.

5. Neatly trimmed nails; neatly manicured or polished for women.

6. Limit jewelry. Avoid wearing anything distracting or memorable.

7. No fragrance.

8. If you're not sure it's appropriate, don't wear it.

9. Be aware of the dress code for the industry in which you're hoping to work and then dress appropriately. A rule of thumb is: Know the code and then take it up a level. This will take some homework on your part.

10. If you're a smoker, don't smoke just before your interview. Do take breath mints along.

So displaying professionalism is about having some level of expertise and it's about looking good—but it's so much more than that. What is professionalism, exactly? I believe that a thorough examination of this word shows it has multiple dimensions, and we've got to understand them all.

PROFESSIONALISM IS A MINDSET

On the day I decided to make professional sports my life's work, I began soaking myself in that world. Whatever it took to be the best, I was going to do it. I've since come to recognize that this is the mindset of a professional.

> *A professional is someone who can do his best work when he doesn't feel like it.*

- A professional is someone who studies the standards, and then seeks to raise the bar.

- A professional is someone who continually develops herself to stay, not on the "cutting edge," but ahead of the pack. I constantly urge our Magic interns to read at least two sports sections every day and read all the national sports magazines every week.

- A professional is someone whose life focus is his field of interest.

- A professional is someone for whom there are no days off from her craft, just occasionally more relaxing days in which to gain perspective.

Think Jack Bauer, without the hard-edged attitude: professionalism is a twenty-four-hour-a-day, seven-days-a-week pursuit. There is no time off. Author Andy Stanley states, "There aren't any time-outs in life. The clock is always ticking."

PROFESSIONALISM IS A STANDARD OF LIVING

A standard is a point of reference against which other things are evaluated, often an ideal by which we judge one thing against another. Standards of living are often measured in terms of relative income levels.

But when it comes to professionalism, the standard of living I'm talking about has more to do with the attitude of pride in what you do than with income, although most "professions" do have an above average salary range. The standard of comparison here has more to do with that mindset of professionalism. There are those who would not consider entering any area of life without displaying professionalism, and there are those who simply don't care at all.

Someone who is not interested in a professional standard of living often has no standards at all. He dresses any way he wants and expects to get paid for his work whether he's done it well or not.

The person who displays professionalism, however, is continually aware that she represents her occupation, company, or field of interest. She considers herself an ambassador of goodwill for that endeavor. She realizes this means she must be on her most exemplary behavior at all times, even in her private life. She carries herself with dignity and treats others with the utmost respect.

Professionalism raises the bar on our standard of living.

PROFESSIONALISM IS AN ACTION

Displaying professionalism is about more than looking good and earning a paycheck. We display professionalism in how we do our jobs and in how we prepare for them. Professional soldiers, for example, are constantly training for whatever battle might come their way. Professional athletes are always on their game. Even when their bodies are at rest, their minds are on the court or in the stadium, picturing that next game and how they can improve on the last one.

Professionals are people who treat one another with respect, who do their best to always be on time, and who live by the highest of ethical standards, both on and off the job.

Professionals are people who study hard, play hard, and work hard. They keep their personal lives separate from work time and they play fair when it comes to office "politics."

Professionals are people who recognize that, even in our politically correct climate, the rules of etiquette have not changed much over the years. They are polite and considerate to everyone they meet, considering the needs of others before their own.

Professionals are people who never gossip or tell tasteless jokes. They are sensitive to the feelings of others.

Professionals are people who think ahead. When uncertain of the appropriate dress, behavior, or response for a pending event, they seek the expertise of others.

Professionals are people who prepare for their job interviews by researching the companies, tailoring their résumés to fit, and who show respect for the interviewer by being on time and looking good.

If the person I've been describing here sounds like you, you'll have no trouble "nailing" that job interview.

YOUR JOB INTERVIEW NAIL GUN:
DISPLAY PROFESSIONALISM

1. Show that you care about the company with whom you're interviewing.

2. Make sure your résumé reflects a constant pattern of growth in your chosen career path.

3. Remember to dress for the job you want, not the one you have or just left.

4. Display a high standard of personal conduct.

5. Let your life reflect professional presence.

CHAPTER 5:

Exude Self-Confidence

In addition to building a personal network, being interview-question ready, being prepared, and displaying professionalism, a fifth universal quality you'll need if you want to nail that job interview is the ability to project an aura of self-assuredness. Sound a little too highbrow for you? Hear me out.

I'm not talking about cockiness or arrogance, but a confidence that exudes from your inner being.

Nor am I talking about self-esteem. Not that many years back, some people were becoming so concerned with bruising someone's sensitive ego they believed it was necessary to issue only positive strokes, no matter how badly the individual had behaved. This was deemed especially true regarding children. But it is utter nonsense! If we have failed at a task or done something we shouldn't do, we need to understand that our behavior was inappropriate. That's how we learn. By failing, we discover who we are, what we do well, and where we need to improve.

When it comes to self-esteem, most of us esteem ourselves much more highly than we ought. After all, who is the first person you look for in a group photograph or a plate glass window as you're walking by? Yes, you may have had a lifetime of negative messages pumped into your head, but don't believe them. You may have had bad things happen in your life. But you can overcome these things. You are strong and capable. I have faith in you. You need to have faith in you too.

Self-confidence is not self-esteem. Self-confidence is an assuredness that says, "I can *do* this."

Motivational speaker Brian Tracy explains it this way: "Whatever we expect with confidence becomes our own self-fulfilling prophecy." It's true. The candidate who expects to get the job—without any show of arrogance—is often the one who is chosen.

YOU CAN DEVELOP SELF-CONFIDENCE

Self-confident? You may be thinking. *That is not me. I fail at everything I do.*

No matter how low your confidence tank may be, the fact is you *don't* fail at everything you do. In fact, you succeed far more than you fail. And when you do occasionally blow it, you learn not to do that again.

Self-doubt is a terrible thing. People who don't believe in themselves . . . you feel like kicking them. You must believe in yourself."

–RAY BRADBURY

"If at first you don't succeed," the old saying goes, "try, try again." We all experience times of failure. Learn to read its message. Is your failure saying *this isn't the direction for you*, or is it saying *try again, but in a different way*? We often become so discouraged by failure that we give up altogether.

Where would we all be if Walt Disney had decided, after old Charles Mintz stole his chief character Oswald and nearly all his artists from him back in 1928, that he should just go into another line of work? We certainly wouldn't be booking trips to Walt Disney World or taking our kids to Hannah Montana movies. Imagine a world with no Mickey Mouse! I can't. But Walt knew the secret—and he called it "stick-to-it-ivity." Walt did not give up. He tried and he tried again. Today his success is legendary. Walt Disney had confidence in his dreams.

General Colin Powell told *Success* Magazine in February 2009, "What you do with a failure is study it and see what you did wrong, what you did to fail in the situation. Once you've analyzed it and learned from it, roll that mistake up and throw it over your shoulder and move on." Staring at your mistakes in the rear view mirror is self-defeating, Powell said,[10] and I concur.

There are ways to grow your self-confidence. That notion we discussed earlier about having daily goals is one tool that helps build self-confidence. You've got to find some way to realize this. Each task you complete brings with it a sense of accomplishment that builds on itself. Take my checklists, for example. Do you know how it grows my self-confidence every time one of my lists is completed? The satisfaction level is unparalleled.

If your job is too big to be done in one day, like losing weight or writing a book, then find some way to measure your progress toward that end. Keep a journal or a daily word goal, something that acts as a mile marker. You'll be amazed at the motivation you'll gain when you do.

As you can imagine, the Williams kids had leadership lessons poured into their young lives. When our youngest, Alan, was in high school, he wanted nothing to do with leadership. Goofing off was good enough for him. One day, as we were driving home from school, Alan said, "Dad, guess what?"

I said, "What, Alan?"

"The coach named me captain of our basketball team today!" he proudly announced.

"That's great, Alan," I replied, and then I went in for the kill. "Guess what that makes you?" I said.

He thought for a minute. "A leader?" he squeaked. That season boosted young Alan's self-confidence more than a hundred lectures from Dad could have ever accomplished.

If you're in need of some self-confidence enhancement, look for things you can do to build that area of your life. Here are a few ideas:

- Go out for some activity you enjoy at school, in your community, or your church. Decide to become a leader when possible. Leading a team heightens your confidence in ways you can't imagine until it happens.

- Listen to motivational speakers and try your hand at writing your own "commercial."

- Get in shape. Taking care of your body always makes you feel better about yourself, so schedule a daily workout.

- Read from the Psalms and/or New Testament – this is a favorite for me. When I put my confidence in God, I become unstoppable.

- Focus on what you can do for someone else.

- Develop an attitude of gratitude.

Notice that these suggestions are mostly pursuits that take the focus off of you and put them on someone or something else. Taking your eyes off yourself is, ironically, one of the first and most critical steps in building self-confidence.

Life is not easy for any of us, but what of that? We must have perseverance and, above all, confidence in ourselves. We must believe that we are gifted for something and that this 'something,' at whatever cost, must be attained.

–MARIE CURIE, NOBEL PRIZE WINNING PHYSICIST

THE SELF-CONFIDENT INTERVIEW

Confidence is defined as a state of being certain, or of having faith in someone or something. Self-confidence indicates certainty and faith in yourself. So how do you display your self-confidence during an interview?

Even if you're a novice, it's important to act like you've been through the interview process before—not by adopting a "been there, done that" attitude, but with the confidence that says you are the right person for this job. You'll feel more sure of yourself if you:

1. Dress well. Remember those tips from the last chapter.

2. Walk with confidence, taking long, strong steps. Be intentional.

3. Compliment people. Be sure you are sincere when you do this and don't go overboard. Phoniness shows.

4. Sit up straight and be attentive.

5. Speak clearly and loud enough to be heard. Try not to mumble or use "uh" or "um" excessively.

6. Thank them for the interview opportunity.

7. Show interest in the company and confidence in what you can do to make a contribution.

8. Create an elevator speech: essentially, you in two minutes. Practice it and be ready to deliver it.

There is a difference between conceit and confidence. Conceit is bragging about yourself. Confidence means you believe you can get the job done.

–JOHNNY UNITAS, LEGENDARY NFL QUARTERBACK

If you're feeling uncertain, practice with a parent or friend. Ask them to play the part of interviewer and take you through the paces. In interviewing, as in basketball, the more you practice, the more likely you are to score.

A SELF-CONFIDENT LIFE

Former NFL coach Bill Callahan noted, "Every day you're in this league, you're in an interview."[11] And every day we're in the game of life, we are being interviewed by those around us, whether we know it or not. What impression are *you* making?

This confidence we've been talking about is more than just a job interview technique. What about when you nail the job interview and actually start the job? Will your self-confidence take you into the office and on up the corporate ladder? It can if you develop a life attitude powered by self-confidence.

Confidence is an inside job. You've got to start by believing in yourself. Confidence gives you an ability to bounce back from a fall—essential for people who've lost a job or lost at a job interview.

What I do know is that inner confidence about one's abilities is not only a golfer's primary weapon, but a person's primary weapon, if only because it's the strongest defense against the enormous pressure the game of golf and the game of life impose on you, once you are in a position to win. When you've done it once, your confidence rises. When you've done it twice or three times, you know that you can do it and you know that you know how to do it, as you are coming down the final stretch.

–JACK NICKLAUS, CHAMPIONSHIP GOLFER

Confidence helps you move on to what is next in your life. Confidence helps you realize where you need to improve. As tennis great Martina Navratilova said, "The better I get, the more I realize how much better I can get."

Everyone struggles with confidence issues somewhere, but we all have to be working on it. The best way to build your confidence is through preparation, and that takes repeated practice and the determination to always be working toward perfection. In public speaking circles they say that the only confident speaker is a prepared speaker. Whenever I'm watching someone lining up to make a key putt on the course or a field goal in an NFL football game, I often wonder, is there confidence under that kind of pressure? Well, there is if you've practiced putting every day or made about 500 field goals. When you are practiced, perfected, and proficient, when you have paid the price, the confidence will be there.

Think about taking your high school or college final exams. If you have worked at it, if you've stayed up with it and over-studied, you have every reason to be completely confident. But if you've cut corners, slacked off, or stayed up all night, even if you've drunk enough coffee to make Jell-O look calm, you are winging it. You'll have zero confidence.

YOUR JOB INTERVIEW NAIL GUN: EXUDE SELF-CONFIDENCE

1. Improve your confidence by learning to accomplish something every day.

2. Practice the many confidence-building strategies outlined in this chapter.

3. Be ready to let the interviewer know you are someone who can do the job.

4. Believe in yourself.

CHAPTER 6:

Exhibit Communication Skills

Nothing will kill an interview faster than poor communication skills. No matter how good you look or how carefully you've planned for the interview, if the first words out of your mouth are unintelligible, fumbling, arrogant, or in any other way less than clean, clear, confident, and crisp—your bacon is likely to be cooked. The rest of the interview will be merely a formality.

Remember that your job during an interview is to convince the interviewer that you are the candidate her business needs to hire. In order to do that, you need to communicate credibly and persuasively. Harvard Business School Professor John P. Kotter tells us, "Without credible communication and a lot of it, the hearts and minds of others are never captured."[12] Anytime you are communicating a message that you want to hit its target, your job is to be winsome, attractive, charming. Life attracts life.

Throughout my career, I've observed first-hand the critical nature of effective communication. Every major league sport has its superstars, but the truth is—winning is not about superstars. Winning is always a team effort that requires an active, accurate, and honest communication system.

In 2005, my son Bobby became the manager of the Washington Nationals farm system. He was just twenty-seven when he got the job, very young, so he asked me, "Dad, what do I need to know for this job?" Since that time I've asked about 1500 coaches, "What are the four keys to being a successful coach?" It's been interesting to see so many of the same answers coming from all these different voices. At the top, right after, "Be yourself," is this: "Be able to communicate at all levels—from your superiors, to the players, to the assistants. You must develop a clear and direct speaking style and be a great listener."

Optimism is your number one message, and after it hope. Without those two qualities, teams won't function well. They won't approach the task with a sense of assurance.

In sports, as in all of life, remember that it's not about superstars—it's about teams that communicate effectively with one another. Only those teams win.

When you go in for your job interview, they won't be looking for a new company celebrity. They'll be looking for a team player—someone who works well with others and isn't out for his or her own glory. Be sure this description fits you. If it doesn't, consider getting an attitude makeover before you start applying for jobs.

I'm not saying you need to suppress any extraordinary abilities you have—that's not it at all. But if you are especially gifted and if your gifts happen to be just what the company needs, let that come out through your résumé. During the interview, your job is to communicate your desire to enhance the team, not to stand out on your own.

Why do effective communications with a team focus matter so much? In a book about the U.S. Coastguard, leadership author Donald T. Phillips wrote: "An effective system of communication is important . . . . For one thing, it gets everybody on the same page. That increases the probability of mission accomplishment. In addition, every good leader knows that not having accurate, up-to-date information can kill any chances of achieving the organization's mission."[13] Establish in the job interview that you are someone the organization can count on to help them accomplish their corporate mission.

If you need to, take a class on speaking or join a writers group. Help yourself out by polishing your skills. Being critiqued by others can be scary, but it's one of the best ways I know to prepare. Record yourself and listen for the weaknesses so you can strengthen them. Figure out how to emphasize the strengths you already have.

Effective teamwork begins and ends with communication. The word, of course, means to convey a message. In order to communicate with your teammates, co-workers, or family, you must ask yourself and one another two critical questions:

• How do we talk to one another?

• How do we listen?

Communication must be taught and practiced in order to bring everyone together as one.

–MIKE KRZYZEWSKI, DUKE UNIVERSITY
BASKETBALL COACH

In order to nail the job interview there are several levels on which you'll need to communicate effectively.

WRITTEN COMMUNICATION

Being able to say what you mean in writing so that the receiver clearly understands your intended message is both fundamental and essential. It's not enough just to issue a directive. You've got to be able to express instructions with enough clarity and detail that there is no mistaking them, yet not so burdened down by words that no one reads them. Where would we be today if our Founding Fathers had not clearly articulated our national documents? Your intentions must be plainly spelled out—in writing.

The pen, they say, is mightier than the sword. It's a true statement. The ideas people communicate with the written word can influence generations to come. Or as Lord Byron once put it, "A drop of ink may make a million think." So why aren't more of us concerned with learning how to write well?

Within twenty seconds from the time I meet you or talk to you on the phone, just by that first look or hearing your voice, I immediately form a strong opinion of you—either a good one, or not so good. Your voice and verbal skills are that vital. If that first reaction is not positive, it's going to take a lot to change it. Every time you pick up the phone, it could be a life-changing experience. You don't know who's on the other end.

So if you want to nail that job interview, you've got to brush up on *all* your communication skills, including the ability to write. You may be conducting your interview verbally, but writing is sure to play a part at some point along the way. Let's consider a few possibilities.

WHAT SHOULD "COVER" LETTERS COVER?

Before you get to the interview, you are likely to have one or more opportunities to correspond with the company whose favor you are seeking. Make sure you know how to spell and write well enough to communicate meaning that motivates action.

Many of the human resources professionals I've spoken with mention the all-important cover letter. Would you believe that this tool could eliminate you from the competition almost before you've sung your first song? Done correctly, however, this critical foot-in-the door instrument can keep you from getting your toes pinched.

One HR manager I interviewed told me, "Employers typically will not seriously consider a candidate who has not provided a cover letter. The cover letter is a way of communicating to a potential employer about the position you are looking for and your specific qualifications for that position. The letter should highlight experience that is most pertinent and will help you stand out from the hundreds of résumés that an employer receives. It can also clarify things that the résumé cannot—gaps in employment, changing career focus, or reentering the job market, for example. The cover letter can explain these situations in a positive way and will show you are being up front about areas that may be questionable. The cover letter needs to grab the employer to want to call you for an interview to learn more about you."

If the prospective employer asks you to mail your résumé, include a well-written cover letter. If you're not sure about your own writing skills, get help, but make sure your letter reflects who you are in every way. For your convenience, I've listed a few resources starting on page 153.

USING EMAIL EFFECTIVELY

In our electronic age, job searches are conducted online every day. So it's possible your first contact with a company may be by email. I cannot stress enough the need to avoid using email slang or text message shortcuts. Your email needs to be as professionally crafted and proofread as your cover letter.

One online search agent offers these tips to keep in mind when submitting your résumé by email:

- Include your name and the position for which you are applying in the subject line of the message.

- Use a simple font, such as Arial or Times New Roman.

- If sending your résumé as an attachment, use your name to name the attached file: i.e., JoeSmith.doc.

- Send your résumé using a personal email account. Using your current business email address is a faux pas.[14]

It's a good idea, also, to submit a hard copy of your résumé in addition to the one you email. This accomplishes two things: it gets your name in front of the hiring manager one more time and it tells them you are serious about getting the job.

Again, use the tools available to you in making your email professional, courteous, and effective. If your spelling is questionable, use your computer's spell-check program. When words themselves fail you, reach for your dictionary or thesaurus.

Communication is one of the most remarkable of humanity's gifts and also the greatest of man's individual fears. All parts of our being—spirit, soul and body—depend on communication to function.

–LYNN WILFORD SCARBOROUGH, AUTHOR[15]

VERBAL COMMUNICATION

If you want to nail the job interview, you need to both write well and speak well. I like to call these assets presentation skills. You are judged immediately by the first words out of your mouth. Author and former congressman Bruce Barton said it well, "Talkers have always ruled. They will continue to rule. The smart thing is to join them."

Interview Angel developer Brent Peterson describes your job during the interview as "inspiring the hiring manager." His innovative interview tool, consisting of a professional-looking padfolio complete with interview advice, tabbed sections, and templates, includes a section offering this sage advice:

"The organization is anxiously waiting to be inspired by a job applicant. Most applicants fail to do so simply because they do not know how.

"When I walk into an interview, I am confident that I will get hired. Just like a stage actor before a play, I know exactly what I am going to do and say."

When you go in for your interview, you are auditioning for a role. So make sure you get your lines right.

Prepare yourself. Know the profile of the position for which you're interviewing. Apply elements of your life plan to it. Ask yourself the questions an interviewer is likely to ask: Why do you want this job? Why do you believe you are the best person for this job? How do you see yourself contributing to the company? How would you handle this situation?

Study the company. Know what they're looking for. "I consistently failed interviews," Peterson offers, "because I was not prepared to discuss the company's needs and to discuss my own stories."

Speaking of stories... as a lifetime coach of young people and as a busy public speaker, believe me when I say storytelling goes a long way toward getting your message across. I'm not quite sure why it works, but it does. Perhaps it's as business consultant John Eldred once told me, "We are hard-wired to retain stories—not PowerPoint, thank goodness."

Communication can either build the trust or erode it. Following through on expectations is what builds the trust. One of the places where it often falls through is that people haven't communicated about expectations.

–LILLY PLATT, PRESIDENT OF LEGATO CONSULTING

In an interview situation, of course, you don't want to go off on a tangent or interject stories that are not relevant to the interview. But you'll want to have a ready reserve of stories to back up the questions and/or statements you're likely to make during the interview.

"In an interview setting," said Peterson, "you need to demonstrate behavior (through your own stories) that is consistent with the responsibilities of the position and culture of the organization." None of this, he says, is difficult if you have prepared your own success stories to answer the potential questions you may be asked. Be ready to let that interviewer know how you would handle a hypothetical situation by describing how you have successfully handled similar situations in the past.

Be ready for your interview. If possible, get a friend to quiz you and practice, practice, practice. The idea is *not* to memorize answers—never do that! Interviewing is a *technique* at which you improve through doing. Interview as often as you can. Even if you are not successful in winning every job, you stand to benefit by increasing your network while polishing your style.

BODY LANGUAGE

Before you've spoken a word, your interviewer is going to be able to tell a lot about you, simply by studying your body language. Are you insecure or cocky? Shy or bold? Those qualities are often instantly obvious by the way we walk, stand, sit, or shake hands.

Try to arrive early enough to give yourself time for a brief, relaxing walk. If it's been cold outside, warm your hands before offering one of them in a handshake. Don't jump up too fast when your name is called or you may come across as over-eager. And by the way, on the handshake it's a good idea to let the interviewer go first, and then shake hands firmly while making direct eye contact.

Body language expert Tonya Reiman writes that walking briskly and with purpose into a room helps overcome nervousness.[16]

You communicate more with your tone of voice than with the actual words. Your tone gives more real indication than your words do, of what you are feeling and thinking. Of course, I don't mean to imply that your choice of words is not important. Both are worth practice and careful attention.

GENE KLANN, LEADERSHIP EXPERT[17]

During the interview, do your best to sit up straight. I know I sound like a grouchy parent here, but slouching is not only bad for your posture—it tells the interviewer you are either lazy or you don't really care about the job.

Keep your hands in your lap or at your sides, but keep your body stance open. Folding your arms across your chest may be comfortable, but it "says" defensive. Leaning in to the conversation indicates interest.

You can improve your body language by becoming aware of it. Take an afternoon and people watch if you can. Study how people use their bodies in a variety of ways and ask yourself what the messages might be. Watch people you admire—leaders, the president of the United States, speakers, even your friends. Study their moves. Is there a pattern that might indicate a technique of some kind?

What matters most is to relax. Too much tension or nervousness will show—and will likely keep you from nailing the job interview. You wouldn't want that company to lose out on a great candidate, so loosen up and let them get to know you, while you, in turn, are getting to know them. After all, the interview is just as much about them as it is about you.

Not long ago, I interviewed a young college graduate who wanted to get into sports. I could see she was nervous. She was bright and sharp, but clearly having trouble breathing and was somewhat shaky. "Are you nervous?" I asked. She wanted to be cool, but admitted, "Yes, I really am."

"Let's start again," I said. "I want you to breathe. The best way to combat nerves is to get your breathing under control. Fill your lungs through your nose, hold it for two seconds, and then let it all out until there's nothing left. Repeat that three or four times. You'll notice your heart rate slow down and an inner relaxation taking over."

I have found more than anything else that this exercise helps get me under control and centered, so whenever you get in a situation where you're feeling panicked or anxious, try it.

Then there's the advice to stretch and get all the kinks out, and that's great to do, too. I always do that before I speak. But I've learned a little trick about how to wake up your face muscles. I call it the Pumpkin/Raisin Drill. Don't let anyone see you or they'll think you're weird, but this is what you do. Stretch out your face muscles as big as you can, like a jack-o-lantern, and think P-U-M-P-K-I-N. Make it big and wide, as wide as you can go. Now scrunch them up real tight: raisin. Repeat this exercise a few times: P-U-M-P-K-I-N/raisin. P-U-M-P-K-I-N/raisin. P-U-M-P-K-I-N/raisin. A few of those and you'll feel like you've been to a salon. Now breathe in, hold for a few seconds, and let it all out. On with the show!

CURTAIN CALL!

Once you've made your appointment, remember to rehearse. But when the time comes, be careful not to come across as "practiced." Does that have your head spinning? Let's put it this way: get yourself as ready as you can, and then just be the best "you" you can be. That's who the company wants to get to know.

After the interview, leave a great impression by communicating your gratitude for the opportunity to interview with them. Send a hand-written thank you note as soon as possible—the next day is ideal. Remember that you never get a second chance to make a first impression.

The genius of communication is the ability to be both totally honest and totally kind at the same time.

–JOHN POWELL, AUTHOR, *The Secret of Staying in Love*

Let's rest for a moment on the topic of that thank you note. As a dad, I hounded my kids to express their gratitude for even the small things done for them by others. It really is important, especially in this day and age when civility seems to have taken a trip to another planet. Relatives are happy to receive those notes, and so are job interviewers. Thank you notes say a lot about the caliber of the gratitude-expresser.

A 2005 *Wall Street Journal* article pointed to the difference a tailored follow-up note can make for the job-seeking candidate. Such a note can help you stand out from the pack for the interviewer who conducts upwards of a dozen or more interviews in a week's time, says author Sarah E. Needleman, who offers these five tips for writing that tailored note:

1. Proofread your note thoroughly. Make sure that it reflects not only correct spelling and punctuation, but the correct name and address for the company and recruiters. One HR representative said she sometimes receives notes addressed to competitors—a gaffe that seals the second-interview fate of the well-intentioned note writer.

2. Use the note as an opportunity to reiterate your best qualities. Think of it as a follow-up sales piece. One interviewer recalled receiving a note from a candidate who took time to restate her connections with editors in her field. That inclusion refreshed the interviewer's memory of her and sent her résumé to the top of the list.

3. Let them know you were listening. If you have anything to add to the conversation you had with the interviewer as a follow-up, let the thank you note be your opportunity to do so, like the candidate who included an article on a service that spoke directly to the company concerns the interviewer had focused on.

4. Reflect your understanding of the company's culture, while keeping it professional. If you've interviewed with a company known for what it produces, don't be afraid to acknowledge that reputation, but be aware that ultimately, the interviewer is interested in your knowledge of business etiquette.

5. Send a note to every executive you met during your interview. Again, be sure to customize them for each individual. It helps to recall something specific you may have discussed.[18]

On this topic of writing thank-you notes, I can't resist sharing with you a story from my friend in Lancaster, Pennsylvania, Ken Hussar, who we met in the first chapter.

In January, 1988, the Orlando Magic flew his wife, Carolyn, and Ken to Orlando to discuss the possibility of making Ken the franchise's public relations executive.

"I vividly remember the trip," Ken told me. "We flew in expecting to be welcomed by the Florida sun, and instead we were rudely met by a record-low 38-degree cold front. Things got better from that point. Team representative John Gabriel met us at the airport and drove us to the Radisson Hotel. When we checked into our room, Carolyn discovered a beautiful bouquet of flowers sent by the team. Nice touch!

"The next day, Carolyn was taken on a house-hunting tour while I visited the Magic offices. We had a great and productive working lunch at Church Street Station with team front office personnel Jack Swope, Dan Durso and Marlin Busher.

"Then I had an impromptu encounter with the team's majority investor, William DuPont. Now here was a man to whom my annual teaching salary was lunch money. I greeted him in my Florida-casual apparel with an enthusiastic, 'Hi, Bill!' and we exchanged pleasantries.

"When I returned home, I typed a letter on 'homemade' business stationery to thank 'Bill' for extending to me the job opportunity and to say how I was looking forward to joining the team. I made a copy of the letter for myself, put the original in an envelope, and mailed it.

"It would have been a good idea to proofread the letter prior to posting it. When, after the fact, I did read it, I was mortified to find two typos—and here I was applying for a job as the team's communications specialist! Computer programmers would call these critical errors. Had it been a baseball team I was candidating for, I would have had my three strikes and been out of there!

"So, my advice to the readers of this book, avoid my faux pas parade: (1) Prepare and rehearse yourself for any contingency; (2) Dress appropriately—not in casual-Friday style;

(3) Do not address the executive on a first-name basis—use Mr., Mrs., or Ms., and (4) Have an English-major-type friend proofread your résumé, cover letter, and any other important correspondence *before* you ship it. Your job could depend on it!"

A TWO-WAY STREET

Communications skills are critical for the interviewer as well. Writing in *Investor's Business Daily*, Morey Stettner advises the potential interviewer to write out questions in advance to avoid asking "leading" questions that actually supply the answer. Set your objective for the interview to keep from getting pulled off track. Listening without interrupting is a skill both parties need to hone. Wait for the person talking to finish, then let a second or two pass before you respond or go on to the next topic. During phone interviews, Stettner advises, let the other person know you're taking notes. He's addressing interviewers in this article,[19] but again this is a great tip for interviewing in general. We all want to know the person we're speaking with is interested in what we have to say. I make it a habit to take notes regularly whenever I hear an interesting insight from someone. I recommend it to you too.

That phone interview, by the way, can be as much of a "make it or break it" moment as your résumé and your in-person interview. Lorisse Garcia told me about a man she once interviewed for an executive position. His anxiety showed through the phone line! "He must have had wooden floors in his house," she said, "because all through the interview I could hear the squeak of his pacing. It was very distracting." Another woman let her cell phone ring and picked up text messages while they talked. Lorisse was not impressed.

When you set up a phone interview, plan to dress for it as if you're doing an in-person interview. Dress up, clean up, look good. It *will* affect your attitude over the phone.

Another phone interview Lorisse recalls was with a man who did beautifully all the way through. She could hardly wait to pass him on to the next level—until she asked if he had any questions for her. "Just one," the man replied, and proceeded to ask her a bizarre and completely out of context question. Not personal or profane—just weird. Figuring it was an anomaly in an otherwise good interview, she decided to pass him on anyway and was stunned when the hiring manager reported him asking the same question. "He did *not* ask that," she replied incredulously, and needless to say, the candidate's opportunity for that job ended immediately.

So when it's your turn, remember that story. Don't ask weird questions, just relevant ones—like how long have you been with the company, or do you like your job? Those are valid questions. Avoid coming off as a mental case. The world does not need any more of those, thank you very much.

I recently learned a new metaphor for life attitudes, and I love it. You can either be a fountain or a drain. The fountain is the person who is continually bubbling up with life and refreshment. The drain on the other hand . . . well, the word pretty much says it. When you go in for that job interview, whether on the phone or in person, I encourage you to be a fountain.

YOUR JOB INTERVIEW NAIL GUN: EXHIBIT COMMUNICATION SKILLS

1. You must master the art of the telephone interview. It's quickly becoming the first-round interview of choice, as companies work to streamline the process. At the end of a workday a short while back, I came upon an exhausted Audra Hollifield, Vice President of Human Resources for the Magic. "I've done twelve phone interviews today for the Magic," she said. "One hour each! And it's all for the purpose of narrowing down the candidate pool. We'll bring in maybe three of those twelve." Remember what I said about making a great phone impression. Your next job may depend on it.

2. Write great cover letters, résumés, and emails. Get help if you need it (see Resources, page 153).

3. Learn to speak with confidence. Let your voice and your words say, "I'm the one for you."

4. Get to know your own past stories so you can tell the interviewer how you would handle future situations.

5. Ask a friend to review your body language. During the interview—in fact, just about all the time—it's important to appear positive and in control.

6. Practice all of the above, and remember to relax.

QUESTIONS TO ANTICIPATE

All too often, interviews leave both parties frustrated. One reason for that is the failure to ask or have adequate answers for the right questions. Here are a few I've gathered over the years that you may want to think about, offered in no particular order:

1. What was the biggest challenge you faced in a previous position and how did you handle it?

2. When you think back over your work life to date, what do you wish you'd done differently?

3. As you consider this job, what do you think will be your greatest challenge and how will you handle it?

4. How would a co-worker describe you?

5. Tell me about how you establish work relationships.

6. How do you handle conflict?*

7. How do you set goals and manage your time? What have you learned that helps you to be more effective on the job?

8. How would your best client describe you? Your worst client? Why?

9. Describe your management philosophy. Make sure you have a definition in mind of what "management" means to you. Interviewers are looking for more

than just new employees—they're often scouting for future leaders as well.

10. What do you want to be doing five years from now? We've covered this elsewhere but it's worth noting that your answer, if you want the job, needs to reflect the company's goals and show your flexibility.

11. Describe how you would motivate people who report to you. Avoid one-size fits all answers, but develop a scenario or two to show how you might handle different individuals.

12. How do you handle change? My research over the past few years has told me that change is right up there with public speaking as a number one fear. The company is going to want to know if you are adaptable or set in your ways—and they're going to want to see flexibility. If change is not currently something you embrace, work on your attitude. Recognize that change should not be simply for change's sake, but to achieve a positive difference.

13. How do you feel about your life so far? Have you made a success of it?

14. What obstacles are likely to trip you up?

15. What things disturb you most?

16. What was the most useful criticism you ever received?

17. What do you like to do in your spare time?

18. How do you get along with people you dislike?

19. How do you spend a typical day?

---

*Don't be afraid to admit past defeats
if you can demonstrate you have
grown and learned from them.*

Mark DiMassimo, CEO of DiMassimo Brand Advertising, offers this sage advice:

"Before anyone gets hired by DiMassimo Brand Advertising, they must be interviewed by me. I don't rush. Sometimes, the interview can take two hours; sometimes it takes more than one interview.

"I have a little test I do with every single applicant. It is simply the most effective question I've found for understanding a potential team member: What gives you satisfaction?

"I hand them a piece of paper and a pencil and I ask them to make a list of ten things they've done in their lives that they remember with satisfaction. I tell them that this shouldn't include 'interview answers' and that 'I broke up with my boyfriend' could be an excellent answer.

"One inflexible rule is that five of the answers must come from before their 18th birthday. These early successes tell a lot.

"For me, it was the short story I wrote in the seventh grade and the effect it had on my parents and the head of the English department at my school. The feeling of power!

"I study these lists, both with the prospective team member and after the interview. I look for themes like courage, creativity, independence, adventure, rebellion, belonging, and discovery. Once I have a sense of a candidate, I can match the satisfaction to the job. This helps not only with hiring, but with every interaction with that team member for as long as we work together. I feel I have a sense, from the beginning, how things will go right and how things could go wrong with this person. It's a good question."[20]

An article in my files from a long lost *Reader's Digest*[21] features another eight questions you're also likely to hear:

1. ***Tell me about yourself.*** Here's where that elevator speech we talked about comes in. Design it to impress favorably and make sure it says, in two minutes or less, why you are the right person for this job. Focus on your strongest skills, key accomplishments,

and personality strengths. At least one note advises keeping your answer to sixty seconds or less.

2. *Why are you in the job market?* Don't hem and haw. Be direct and prompt in answering this question.

3. *What can you do for us?* Make sure you've researched the company and the position, then give them your best answer.

4. *What are your strengths?* Are you high energy, enthusiastic, assertive, decisive, mature? Do you get results? Resist the temptation to answer, "I can do whatever you need me to do." Be as specific as you can be.

5. *What are your weaknesses?* If possible, try to give an example that is really an overuse of a strength. For example: "Sometimes people think that because I'm quiet I'm not engaged. I've learned to get my ideas across through actions that show I'm paying attention and I care about the results." Do your best to show you have learned from past mistakes.

6. *What type of boss do you like?* This question seeks to know whether or not you're likely to have conflicts. Why not say: "I like a competent and strong leader I can learn from who will let me take chances but coach and mentor me when I need it"?

7. ***What are your most significant achievements?*** List the highlights you're most proud of over the past five years.

8. ***What salary are you looking for?*** Do your best to give a range that shows you're negotiable. Avoid lowballing, which shows a lack of confidence, or highballing, as that could scare the employer off.

And if you're the interviewer, you'll want to study the interviewee's character to discover if the applicant:

1. Would work well in the face of opposition.

2. Is excitable or even-tempered.

3. Is impatient or understanding.

4. Has the ability to plan.

5. Is likely to work to correct weaknesses.

6. Is a leader or a follower.

CHAPTER 7:

Radiate Energy and Enthusiasm

A radio interviewer asked me recently, "Where do you get all the energy to do everything you do?" I laughed, but understood his question. As a man who's a sports executive, father of nineteen, devoted husband, author, marathon runner, and on-the-go public speaker, I'm often asked this question. I'm also nearly seventy years old—an age many of you might regard as ready for the front porch rocker. Well, that scenario is not for me. All of us are getting older, every second we draw breath. There is no magic age at which older equals giving up. I believe in wearing out rather than rusting out. So I told the interviewer, "I think energy is a choice. Some people think it's an emotion, but I think every day you can decide to be enthusiastic and energetic."

I've learned throughout my busy life that energy and enthusiasm carry the day. People celebrate life when they see it. And nowhere is this truer than in the job interview.

I'm not saying you have to come on like the Sham-Wow guy, but conveying a natural, healthy energy is going to take you far. If that sounds like a stretch for you right now, if you're having difficulty just making the trip from the sofa to the refrigerator—the good news is that you can make a turn in the right direction, starting right now.

Remember that life plan we talked about in chapter two? Wherever you want to go in life, you're going to need a lot of energy to get there. Would those who know you well describe you as an energetic person? Author Jon Meacham wrote of Winston Churchill, "What you saw was usually what you got… a big, boisterous, occasionally overbearing bundle of energy."[22] Is that you? What would others say? If winning a job interview is on your wishlist, you'll need to focus on developing this essential life force.

Merriam-Webster defines *energy* as "1 a: dynamic quality b: the capacity of acting or being active c: a usually positive spiritual force; 2: vigorous exertion of power: effort; 3: a fundamental entity of nature that is transferred between parts of a system in the production of physical change within the system and usually regarded as the capacity for doing work; 4: usable power (as heat or electricity); also : the resources for producing such power."[23]

Energy and persistence conquer all things.

–BENJAMIN FRANKLIN

If we boil that definition down to a few keywords I think the picture becomes clearer. Energy equals dynamism, activity, positive force, and power. Those are all qualities I want to be known for. Don't you? So how do we get there?

Oprah Winfrey is often quoted as having said, "Energy is the essence of life. Every day, you decide how you're going to use it, by knowing what you want and what it takes to reach that goal and by maintaining focus." There's that choice again. Energy comes from the decisions we make, every day.

Remember our checklist of daily goals? These are triggers that jumpstart energy. I believe energy and purpose go hand-in-catcher's glove. When you know your purpose, either in life or in the moment, the energy to accomplish what needs to be done just comes naturally. It was Dr. Norman Vincent Peale, the original positive-thinker, who said, "The more you lose yourself in something bigger than yourself, the more energy you will have." Well said, Dr. Peale. Well said.

CHOOSE ENERGY FOR LIFE

Have you ever heard people reply, when asked how they feel, "I couldn't be better if I were twins!"? Well, the truth is we all need to be like quadruplets when it comes to energy, focusing on all four areas of our being: physical, mental, social, and spiritual. Choosing energy comes naturally when these four are in balance.

Do you find yourself waking up every day joyfully exclaiming, "Oh, good! It's morning, God!" Or are you more likely to groan out, "Oh, good God, it's morning"? I'd venture to say that many of us dread morning. But think of it this way: each day is like a blank scoreboard, with no goose eggs on it yet. So what can we do to encourage our bodies to wake up refreshed and ready to go? I believe there are a few pathways to explore—and all of them will help us nail our next job interview.

In life, what you need is horsepower.
What I had, I used.

–KATHRYN HEPBURN

EAT FOR ENERGY

One way to increase energy is through your food choices. Nothing beats fresh fruit, vegetables, and water for keeping the body humming along as it was meant to do. After all, our bodies were made to run on these good, nutritious whole foods, and these foods were made for our bodies. It's a natural set-up. If you fill your tank everyday with these delicious biofuels, your engine will purr and your personal mpg will break records. It's only when we gunk up the system with over-processed, sugary, or starchy foods that we begin to develop engine trouble and end up in the shop.

And boring though it sounds, water is really the only fluid our bodies need. I believe that if you commit to drinking water more than any other beverage, in time you'll crave the water and bypass the soda. Water is, after all, what the Designer recommends. Substitutes should be limited. Personally, I can't think of anything more refreshing on a hot Florida day than an ice-cold bottle of H20. In fact, I think I'll go grab one right now.

ENERGY BEGETS ENERGY

Physical fitness is another key to becoming a fountain of energy. I know, you've heard it so many times you could scream. But you really do need a regular fitness program. If you don't already have one, please put finding one at the top of your to-do list.

Our bodies were made to move. We've been given limbs with moving joints that can transport us magically from one place to another. Today's world, however, makes it necessary for us to use machines for transportation—cars, airplanes, buses, and trains. Our jobs tether us to desks and computers all day long. As a result, few of us walk as much as we should.

But all of us can do more. We can find and start a new daily routine that includes vigorous physical exercise. I like to run, and I do it every day. Find something you enjoy. It might be jogging, cycling, walking the dog, or swimming. Whatever it is, do it regularly.

On April 23, 2009, FoxNews reported on a study that claims those who spend more time sitting than standing or moving around are likely to have less time on this planet. Dr. Melina Jampolis told FoxNews that this study followed more than 17,000 people for over twelve years and found that people who spend the majority of their time sitting increase their chances of dying during that time by fifty percent![24] In our computer generation, I know we can all relate to increased time sitting. There are many things you can do to conquer these statistics.

If you sit at a desk all day, set a timer to go off every hour. Then get up and walk around. Do some stretches. One associate of mine has placed a rebounder in the corner of her office and every hour she does a gentle two-minute bounce. A simple activity like that works out every cell in the body every hour, revitalizing the heart, the brain cells, you name it. Moving our bodies is also the key to burning fat, and most of us can use a little help in that department.

Think of your body as a rechargeable battery. It must be discharged before it can be recharged. And then it must be connected to an energy source to be reinvigorated. Exercise is a great energy source.

The only thing that keeps a man going is energy, and what is energy but liking life?

–LOUIS AUCHINCLOSS, NOVELIST AND HISTORIAN

ENERGY DEFINES LEADERSHIP

One purpose I believe all people have is to see themselves as leaders. Oh, it's true enough that there are natural leaders and natural followers. I'm not arguing that point. But every one of us is influencing someone else's life, and that's what a leader does. A leader is an influencer. Does that word "influence" illustrate how you see yourself? I hope so, because leaders are always energetic people. Their passion energizes them.

John C. Maxwell compares leaders to locomotives, in that both are a "source of energy and direction."[25] When it comes to your job search, try to think of yourself as a locomotive. It's your energy driving the search and your energy that will nail the interview. Your energy, plus one more essential ingredient: enthusiasm.

THE MIND GAME

The word "enthusiasm" comes from a Greek word meaning, "be inspired." It is defined as 1) a feeling of excitement; 2) overflowing with eager enjoyment or approval; 3) a lively interest.[26] We are enthusiastic about that which has captivated our hearts and minds. Enthusiasm, then, is the mental aspect of energy. It's what inspires you to get going and get things done.

When it comes to the job interview, we need to display enthusiasm for the company and job we are hoping to nail. But more important is being an enthusiastic person.

I have authored a number of books with Michael Mink, who, over the years, has written over 400 articles for the Leaders and Success page in *Investor's Business Daily* (by the way, that page is a must read for anyone who wants to live life to its fullest). I asked Michael what was the common trait he'd found that ran through all these famous people he has interviewed and researched and written about. Michael answered immediately, "They all had passion in their chosen field that was absolutely off the charts."

When I think of the word "enthusiasm" many images come to mind, but few exceed the natural passion of my young friend and partner in publishing this book, Adam Witty. Adam is zeal personified, and it's more than just his 6'6" frame. He is passionate about his work, engaged and active in more areas than fleas on a dog, a true lover of life. If his energy holds out another fifty or sixty years, I believe he could be lethal—and I mean that in all the good ways.

I studied the lives of great men and famous women, and I found that the men and women who got to the top were those who did the jobs they had in hand, with everything they had of energy and enthusiasm and hard work.

–HARRY S. TRUMAN, 33RD U. S. PRESIDENT

My personal regimen for daily energy has served me well for lo, these many years, and it just might benefit you too. In addition to my morning run, I start out my day with uplifting thoughts from the Bible, a nutritious breakfast, an intense weight-lifting session, and time spent with those who matter most in my life—my wife and family. If I'm away from home, as I often am, I pick up the phone just to say, and hear, "I love you." We all need a lift in the morning and this routine energizes my day like nothing else I've tried.

IT'S WHO YOU ARE

Jeffrey A. Krames, business author and editorial director of the Portfolio imprint for The Penguin Group, summarizes the topic of this chapter beautifully when he writes:

"Strictly defined, energy means a source of power, whether electrical, mechanical, or otherwise. But for our purposes, there is more to energy than its physical properties. In addition to physical energy, there is also mental energy and what might be called 'emotional energy'—the kind of energy that a leader projects to help build the spirit or morale of an organization [sic].

"It is an energy that reaches across people and binds together individual contributions into a purposeful whole. In that sense, emotional energy can be as important as or more important than physical energy. Emotional energy is the passion that gets the job done."[27]

Put your personal passion to work for you during the job interview. Display energy. Keep an open posture. Make good eye contact. Let the interviewer see that you have a keen interest in the job and the industry. You don't have to jump around like a miniature poodle, but don't be afraid to let your *natural* enthusiasm show.

Ultimately, I agree fully with nineteenth century Scottish author and reformer Samuel Smiles, who concluded, "It is energy . . . the central element of which is will . . . that produces the miracle that is enthusiasm in all ages. Everywhere, it is what is called force of character and the sustaining power of all great action."

Energy and enthusiasm go together like the basketball and LeBron James. Put them both to work for you, and you'll score every time. It all comes back to the will.

The key is to be strong and passionate, but relaxed. At first it might take a little practice, but if you determine to learn it, that attitude will be for you as second nature as it is for me. And one day people will be asking you, "Where do you get all that energy?" And you can tell them!

YOUR JOB INTERVIEW NAIL GUN: RADIATE ENERGY AND ENTHUSIASM

1. Improve your diet: choose fruits, vegetables, and water whenever possible.

2. Find a physical activity you enjoy and do it every day. Don't make the mistake of sitting at your desk all day afterwards, either. Take time out every hour to move.

3. Find inspiration to jumpstart your day, every day. It all goes back to your purpose.

4. Let your personal passion drive the day.

CHAPTER 8:

Reveal Your Extraversion

What is "extra-version"? No, it's not the annotated news, nor is it an additional rendition of an old favorite. Rather it's a term that applies to people who are typically energized by social involvement, active, and engaged with life. An extravert, sometimes spelled "extrovert," is the opposite, of course, of the introvert, or the person who is withdrawn from life. Which one are you?

The folks at Meyers-Briggs, who create personality assessment tests, say that "extraversion vs. introversion" comprises the first of four pairs of psychological preferences all of us have.[28] They say that everyone spends time both extraverting and introverting. And I suppose that's true. Even I, a lifelong people collector, enjoy being alone with a good book for at least part of my day.

The determining factor as to which of these two preferences dominates in your life is where you find your energy. Are you energized by being around people and involved in people-related activities? If so, you tend toward extraversion. If, on the other hand, you draw energy from hibernating at a computer desk or contemplating life from your favorite quiet place, you favor introversion. Now, we extraverts have difficulty accepting this truth, but it's a fact that one is not better than the other. Both have their place in this world.

When it comes to the job interview, however, you want to do your best to let the extravert in you shine through. Even if you are an introvert by nature, you can learn to manifest extravert traits when you need them.

THE INTROVERT'S EXTRAVERSION

My partner in writing this book told me, "Until I took a job in retail, I had a hard time 'going first' when it came to introducing myself to others. One day I was instructed, 'Say *hello* to people when they come into the store. Ask what you can help them find,' and that challenge became a key that helped turn me inside out. Since that job, I've had no trouble being extraverted in that way." When you put yourself in another's place, when you recognize that in any relationship someone has to initiate contact, you can learn to be an extravert.

As a child I was very introverted, often spending my time on the computer, reading, playing video games, or pursuing other solo hobbies . . . . However, over a long period of time, I eventually found myself becoming more and more extroverted. I embraced spending time with other people, went out of my way to meet new people, could comfortably introduce myself to strangers, and actually enjoyed it. The Myers-Briggs test now labels me an extrovert. To the people who know me today, this wouldn't be surprising.

STEVE PAVLINA, SELF-HELP GURU, "HOW TO
GO FROM INTROVERT TO EXTROVERT"[29]

Many people with naturally introverted personalities manage to come across as "go-getters" or as "people-people" because they learned to enjoy working on teams or in groups. Not only have they found it agreeable, but they've cultivated a wide circle of friends.

I know you can learn it, because I've seen others do it—like my son Bobby. Not to pick on Bobby here, but this story illustrates my point well. Bobby has always had a great love for baseball and has made his living in that world for the past decade. Bobby is by nature shy and somewhat introverted. Realizing the importance of getting to know people, I've always encouraged him to approach and be approachable, to strike up conversations and seek opportunities to connect with others. Now in his early thirties, he's made dramatic strides. He is far more comfortable initiating conversations. Bobby sees that baseball is all about people and relationships. If we're going to succeed in the business of collecting people, I think we all have a certain shyness to overcome. It can be uncomfortable meeting people the first time. *What if they don't like me? Maybe they'll think I'm a pest.* It's a daily discipline to fight through the butterflies and qualms. Force yourself into action. It is a skill, and no matter what your nature—whether you're the introvert or the extravert—you can learn it.

Again, I am not saying the introvert does not have equal value in life. Remember, we are talking about winning the job interview here. The person who is outgoing in the interview is more likely than the wallflower to be hired.

Being an introvert, by the way, does not have to mean being antisocial. No matter how you have seen yourself in the past, these are the true facts about you:

1. You are a unique individual. There has never been anyone like you ever before and there never will be again. You are it. A one-of-a-kind designer original.

2. You have qualities within you that are meant for you to use in helping others. Perhaps you have a gift of encouragement or an ability to feel compassion for others or a natural leadership bent. Don't keep these gifts to yourself—that's not why you have them.

3. Your abilities set you apart from the crowd. Whatever you're naturally good at doing, build that up. Develop it. Add to your skill sets and make yourself someone the right employer can't afford not to hire.

4. Don't think that area about which you feel most passionate is simply meant to be a hobby or something your pursue "someday." Maybe, just maybe, there is a way to do that thing you love and get paid for it. As I've always said, "Find a way to get paid for doing what you love and you'll never work a day in your life."

5. Your life is not simply about today, but is a combination of every experience you've ever had. Put those experiences to work for you in becoming the best "you" you can be. Even past pain can make you a better, stronger person if you find a way to slide it into your win column.

EXTRAVERSION INSPIRES OTHERS

In the job interview, revealing your extraverted side is critical. Determine to convey your sense of adventure and share those experiences that have allowed you to live life to the fullest.

Interview Angel's Brent Peterson identifies five tips as most important in creating that inspiration:

1. **Identify the needs of others** – During the interview, Peterson suggests, encourage the interviewer to talk about their needs and interests. Limit your own talking to no more than half the conversation.

2. **Tell relevant stories** – You will likely be asked to demonstrate behavior consistent with the position

and company culture for which you are interviewing. Prepare an arsenal of success stories in which you describe the situation you were in, your goals within the job, the action you took in the situation, and the results of your action. Make sure your stories have positive outcomes.

3. **Keep it simple** – Avoid boring or confusing the interviewer with lengthy stories about yourself; keep questions straightforward. Don't ask questions that take a lot of thought or time to answer.

4. **Show gratitude** – Without fawning, let the interviewer know you are grateful for the opportunity to meet with his or her company, for taking time to get to know you. The easiest way to make this happen is by developing a life attitude of gratitude.

5. **Take action** – During the interview, act as you would if you were on the job. Be prepared, act in a professional manner, and follow through.[30]

Each of these five tips involves thinking outside yourself—and that is one way to spell "extraversion."

INCREASING CONNECTION

Practicing your extraversion is also a pathway for increasing your connections with others who may be able to help you land your next job or the one after that. In his Leadership Wired newsletter, leadership guru Dr. John C. Maxwell outlines eight tips for connecting with people. I believe these will work on any level. Fold these concepts into your own life and watch them bring out, not only the extravert in you, but the very best in others:

1. **Don't take people for granted** – Remember that results happen through relationships.

2. **Possess a difference-maker mindset** – Seek to influence and inspire others.

3. **Initiate movement toward people** – Break through fear and self-doubt by being willing to make the first move. Be someone who rouses others to action.

4. **Search for common ground** – No matter what the overall objective of any conversation, the best way to initiate it is to find common ground. Look for places of common agreement or interest.

5. **Recognize and respect differences** – Realize that we are all different and learn to make those differences complement one another rather than clash.

6. **Learn the key to others' lives** – As you get to know people, try to identify their inner passion. Once you see it, use that knowledge to benefit him or her and not yourself.

7. **Communicate from the heart** – Make sure your words match your actions. Be passionate about what matters to you.

8. **Share common experiences** – Meeting together for meals or ballgames builds connection.[31]

YOUR JOB INTERVIEW NAIL GUN: REVEAL YOUR EXTRAVERSION

1. Practice being outgoing, even if that trait does not come naturally.

2. Remember that there is only one "one-and-only" you.

3. Focus on the needs of the company.

4. Keep your answers and your questions brief and to-the-point.

5. Let your interview be a "connecting with people" life episode.

CHAPTER 9:

Have Integrity

Few men have been so closely identified with integrity as America's sixteenth president, Abraham Lincoln. Many decades after his passing, we still call him "Honest Abe." So much did integrity mean to Lincoln he would advise young lawyers, "If, in your own judgment, you cannot be an honest lawyer, resolve to be honest without being a lawyer. Choose some other occupation, rather than one in the choosing of which you do, in advance, consent to be a knave." He believed in telling the truth and in being honest with people. That is the heart and soul of integrity. It's about walking what you talk; being a living example of what you say you believe.

The word "integrity" comes from the Latin root word "integer," which means whole, or undivided. Integrity, then, describes what is unbroken, wanting nothing, or morally sound.

I've been fortunate in my life to know coach John Wooden, who's approaching his ninety-ninth birthday as I write. Year-after-year, Coach Wooden led UCLA basketball teams to winning championship seasons. A few years ago, I wrote a book about him called *How to Be Like Coach* (HCI, 2006), for which I interviewed hundreds of people who knew him well. Over and over again came the examples of integrity. It's a constant in Coach Wooden's life.

One story in particular involved Lorenzo Romar, head basketball coach at the University of Washington. One day he and a few others enjoyed a long visit with Coach at his Encino, California condominium. After they'd left, Coach noticed some loose change had slipped out of someone's pocket and fallen into his sofa. Coach retrieved the change and tracked down Romar to find out how he could return it to its rightful owner. To this day, Romar is still blown away by that memory. In Coach Wooden's mind it is written in steel that talk and action must match. Integrity to him is a more all-encompassing word than honesty. You can be honest and lazy, he points out, or honest and undisciplined, or honest and a gossip. You can be honest and lots of things. Your reputation is what people think you are. Your character, Coach says, is who you really are. It's good to have a good reputation, but you can mask that. You can't mask your character. For that, you must have integrity.

The candidate who displays integrity in the job interview is the man or woman who already *is* a person of integrity. Let's take a look at the character qualities a person of integrity possesses.

PEOPLE WITH INTEGRITY ARE HONEST

For people with integrity, honesty is second nature. To be less than honest at all times is something the person of integrity cannot fathom. Here, Lincoln said, "I have always wanted to deal with everyone I meet candidly and honestly. If I have made any assertion not warranted by facts, and it is pointed out to me, I will withdraw it cheerfully."

Being honest does not mean you are always right. It is impossible for us to be right all the time. Nothing wrong with that, it's just a consequence of being human and living in a broken world. But when we are revealed to be wrong, we must admit it, 'fess up and come clean. That is being honest. Never fudge on your résumé. It's so easy to check it out. More people get in trouble by saying they have a degree they don't have. Don't you do that! With all the modern technology available today, everything about you can be easily checked out. If you claim anything that's not true, it can be easily verified. And then what would you do? If they challenge you, what would you say? Your goose would be cooked for that interview and possibly quite a few more after that. Don't try to take credit for something in life that you haven't done—a degree you haven't earned, work you never put in, honors you never received. It's awfully easy to say, "I've got a Master's"—but it takes two years to earn one. Don't take someone else's work away from them through your dishonesty. If that's not a tip off of who you are, I don't know what else is—and I know you are better than that.

In preparation for your job interview, do a little soul-searching. Are you a person who is always honest? If the answer is, "well, mostly," please realize that "mostly" is not good enough. You must determine to be a person who is honest *all* the time. Any employer will expect that. We all want to work with people we can trust.

Integrity is honesty—with a little oomph.

-MICHAEL WILLIAMS, THE AUTHOR'S SON

Now being honest does not mean you have to be like Jim Carrey's character in the movie *Liar, Liar*. You don't need to blurt out everything you are thinking and feeling every moment of the day. Realize that diplomacy is also called for and hold back if your words might offend or hurt someone's feelings unnecessarily—especially if you would simply be expressing an opinion. Every husband whose wife ever asked, "Honey, does this dress make me look fat?" has had to figure this one out. Do you *need* to utter the words? If so, then say what must be said as gently and lovingly as possible. If not, keep your opinion to yourself.

Facts, on the other hand, have a way of coming out. I've found it's always best to get them on the table right away—a lesson many politicians would do well to learn. Don't let anyone ever accuse you of covering anything up.

How can you show yourself to be an honest person in a job interview? Here's where you'll likely want a story in your portfolio, a "for instance" to share when asked. It's not about bragging, just being honest.

But there is more to integrity than just honesty. The late Branch Rickey, legendary major league baseball executive, said this when asked what it takes to prosper as a world-class baseball executive: "I look, first, for integrity. That is a stronger word than mere honesty. It means refusal to trim, cut corners, or seek unfair advantage. It eliminates the fellow who may be legally honest, but who makes sharp deals."

PEOPLE WITH INTEGRITY ARE UNDIVIDED

Confucius, the oft-quoted Chinese philosopher who was rarely confused, said, "Men of principle are sure to be bold, but those who are bold may not always be men of principle."

Integrity is revealed when we take a bold stand for what we believe to be right. Our founding fathers were excellent examples of this quality. Men of diverse backgrounds who were not, as many believe, solidly united in their views, they sought areas of common ground based on universal principles of natural law. In the end, their mutual commitment to doing the right thing led them to establish, as our pledge of allegiance declares, "one nation, indivisible."

That's a great way to live in your own life. Be indivisible. Know what you stand for, be as sure as you can be that you are right, and when you are challenged, be bold in defending your values. If a time comes when you see things a different way, bring in that honesty factor and admit your change of heart and mind.

Jesus said it long ago: "Every kingdom divided against itself will be ruined, and every city or household divided against itself will not stand" (Matthew 12:25 NIV). The great nineteenth century preacher Charles Spurgeon explained, "A united heart is life to a man, but if the heart be cut in twain, in the highest, deepest, and most spiritual sense, he dies."[32]

When you live with an undivided heart, you'll gain the high opinion of others. And you'll deserve it.

Integrity demands unshakeable morals and principles. Remain true to yourself and never compromise your standards.

–R. MATTHEW AMBOY[33]

PEOPLE WITH INTEGRITY ARE TRUSTWORTHY

As general of the American forces, George Washington hungered after the company of those in whom he recognized shared beliefs, the love of what America represented. In evaluating candidates for promotion to higher position, his standards were high. "In every nomination," he said, "I have endeavored to make fitness of character my primary object."

Things haven't changed much in the 200-plus years since Washington's time. We still look for people of integrity to be our leaders: people who are honest, whose passions are undivided, people who are worthy of our trust.

On the battlefield, you've got to be able to trust those around you. That's not just a good idea—it's a necessity. Washington knew that, and so he sought out men he could trust, men who would accept his leadership and trust him in turn.

The same is true in the corporate world, where we must know that the people around us have both the company's and the individual's best interests in mind. Those who seek to serve only themselves ultimately come to ruin. If you need a recent example, think of Bernie Madoff. This man you likely never heard of before late 2008 lived in luxury for years—on money he swindled from others. And now his life will end in a prison cell. Integrity matters. Trust must be earned.

The employer with whom you interview is looking to hire people he can trust—people who will turn in exemplary work performance and who will handle the company's property in a responsible way. People he would be proud to have represent the company. You, as the candidate, want the employer to be trustworthy as well. All too often job offers turn out to be scams. How can you know the difference? People of integrity can often spot the phonies, both coming and going.

No matter what your life story has been up to now, determine from this day forward to be someone others can trust. That way you are likely to have a few stories to choose from when it comes time to demonstrate your integrity to the job interviewer.

PEOPLE WITH INTEGRITY DO THE RIGHT THING

Integrity means having the instincts to know what is right, and then to follow them with all your heart. It begins with your personal worldview. People of integrity tend to believe that life is not about "me," but that they are simply part of a much bigger story. They believe we are all created with equal opportunity. This worldview makes them people who treat life with gratitude. Life for them has a purpose, not just for today but for all eternity. They live by a moral code that is inviolable, not based on the changing whims of public sentiment, but on something lasting and outside themselves. People with integrity treat others with integrity as well.

The most popular lookup for the Merriam-Webster Online Dictionary [in 2005] was the word integrity. The definition given is: "firm adherence to a code of especially moral or artistic values." It's used to describe those who are unwilling to be bribed or morally corrupted. Why was that word on the top of the list? Could it be because integrity is so lacking that many don't know what it looks like in someone's life?

–ANNE CETAS, AUTHOR[34]

Former Arkansas governor Mike Huckabee writes, "Treating people with integrity and respect is the only way to get them to achieve their full potential . . . . Character does count. Integrity does count, but, if integrity and character are divorced from God, they don't make sense. If you try to set your own moral thermostat, chances are that a lot of other people will be uncomfortable. Integrity, left to define itself, becomes evil, because everyone ends up choosing his own standards."[35]

Integrity stands out as a character trait because it has become so rare in our culture. Our headlines are filled with stories of scandal and corruption and other acts done by people who believe integrity is for others, or for a time gone by. But that's not true. People have struggled with doing the right thing since God first gave us a choice. Wrestle with choices if you must, but as much as it's up to you, let the right thing win.

When it comes to getting ready for your job interview, be truthful on your résumé. Be honest in your cover letter. Reveal yourself as someone with unity of purpose. Show yourself as trustworthy on the job. Let the interviewer know you're someone he can trust to always choose the right thing.

People care about character—especially in the workplace. In my world of professional sports, integrity—and the lack thereof—is on display almost daily. Fortunately, I know the majority of professional athletes to be men and women of the highest moral character. But all it takes is one headline to throw suspicion on all the rest.

Don't you be one of those headlines. No employer wants to think she's surrounded by people she can't trust, or even by a rogue employee who might bring her reputation down by stealth behavior.

When you go in for that job interview, you must recognize that you are potentially in the initial bonding stages of life-long relationships. First impressions matter. If you land the job, you'll be engaging with people in the workplace whose respect you'll want to earn and keep.

Character means doing the right thing
when no one is there to see, as well as
when your actions are visible or will likely
be revealed to the world at large.[36]

–STEPHEN H. BAUM, LEADERSHIP EXPERT AND AUTHOR

In a day and age when the ethics of our leaders in both the political and corporate worlds are often questionable at best, being a person of integrity remains a key value. Be someone who makes a difference by choosing personal conduct that reinvigorates and renews the professional landscape.

Berkshire Hathaway CEO Warren Buffett has written, "In looking for people to hire, you look for three qualities: integrity, intelligence, and energy. If they don't have the first, the other two will kill you."[37] If you want the job, *be* a man or woman or integrity.

YOUR JOB INTERVIEW NAIL GUN: HAVE INTEGRITY

1. Be a person of integrity, both in and out of the job interview arena.

2. Realize that honesty matters in the workplace, as it does on every level of your life. Your employer and your coworkers must be able to trust in you.

3. Resolve to be united in your decision-making. Know what you believe and live it.

4. Make it a life goal to be someone others can trust— with their property, with their personal information, and in every area of interpersonal relationships.

5. Make up your mind this minute to always, always, always—do the right thing.

COMMON HIRING MISTAKES

As every employer and HR professional knows, the road to hiring good people is often riddled with potholes. By knowing a few of the common ones[38] in advance, you can avoid being one.

1. **Mistaking charm for competence.** Certain kinds of people have all the right skills to come across well in an interview. They're charming, funny, good with people, and on and on. While these skills may be important, they ultimately will not make up for the qualifications to fill the position.

2. **Talking too much.** Avoid long conversations about yourself (no matter which side of the conversation you're on).

3. **Hiring too fast.** It's tempting to take the first qualified person who walks through the door just so you can end the interviewing process. It's really not unlike dating! But in both cases, you're likely to regret a hasty choice.

4. **Not following up on references.** As an interviewer, don't make this lazy mistake. It's way too easy for people to lie. If you're the job candidate, make sure you have solid, reliable references. Don't fabricate anything! I can't emphasize this point enough. It simply never works, not to mention what it says about you.

CHAPTER 10:

Reveal Creativity

Have you ever heard someone say, "I don't have a creative bone in my body"? It's not true! We are *all* creative, often much more so than we might, ahem, imagine.

Kevin Rafferty of Disney Imagineering put it this way, "[Creativity is] a natural part of your being. Like everyone else on this planet, you were born with the gift of being creative and probably had a joyous time with it until you started to 'grow up.' That's when you put this gift back in the box, much like a toy you were getting too old to play with."[39] Is that how it's been for you? If so, then now is the time to rediscover your inner child.

If you need inspiration, just walk outside and look around. Not at the buildings, but at the trees, the sky, the birds, the flowers—the unending palette of nature. You were made in the image of that Creator! Does that idea thrill you? It does me. What's more, it tells me I have a responsibility to unleash my creative side.

EVERYDAY CREATIVITY

But Pat, I hear some of you saying, *I am not an artist. Even my stick figures are embarrassed by my lack of ability.* Believe me, there are many ways to display our creative intelligence:

- Discovery – Every new realization is an expression of creativity. Whether you are a Christopher Columbus, exploring uncharted territory, or a student realizing what makes math work, you are expressing creativity. Each time you gain a new insight, you are exercising your creativity. And I recommend daily exercise.

- Problem Solving – Believe it or not, problems are opportunities. Without problems, how would we find solutions? Right now, your problem is landing your next job. Reveal your creativity through fresh thinking or examples of past strategies that worked in tight situations.

- Cooking a meal – Even the most bland taste buds get bored with the same thing every day. That's how recipes are developed—and if cooking is a specialty for you, carry that creative thinking into your job interview. I'll bet you can add a few ingredients no one has thought of before.

Creativity everywhere is the best guarantee of future success.

–NIGEL PAINE, FORMER HEAD OF PEOPLE
DEVELOPMENT FOR THE BBC[40]

There are so many ways we express our creativity, in addition, of course, to the more obvious gifts involving the arts: painting, drawing, sculpting, crafts, writing, photography, directing, musical expression and so many more. The outlets are only limited by our imaginations.

So in the job interview, while you don't want to come off as completely wacky (unless, of course, you are interviewing with Ringling Bros.), don't be afraid to let the interviewer know you have a creative side. If you have examples to show, consider bringing along a portfolio of pieces you're willing to leave behind.

When we started the Orlando Magic team back in the late 1980s, people were coming out of the walls looking for jobs. The résumés were flying in left and right. But there was one that stood out. One creative young man had laboriously written out his entire résumé on a basketball. It was nothing short of an artistic masterpiece. Without a doubt, this was the most creative résumé I ever received and I still remember it twenty years later. I kept that basketball a long time.

What can you do that will make you memorable in all the good ways? I know you can think of something.

FEED YOUR BRAIN

When we think of creative "brains"— those people known for great discoveries and inventions—probably the first name that comes to many of us is that of Albert Einstein. And Einstein himself once said, "I did not discover relativity by rational thinking alone." We all have a slightly illogical side, a goofy side, a fun side, a fresh and uninhibited side that we need not tap into now and then.

Over my years in professional sports, I've gained something of a reputation for zany promotions. For that, I credit in a large way my friendship with the legendary Bill Veeck, owner during his lifetime of the Cleveland Indians, the St. Louis Browns, and the Chicago White Sox. To this day, no one has really matched Veeck's craziness on the ball field. Or to put it this way—many of the things he did, which seemed outlandish at the time, have since become accepted elements of the show: fireworks, water-works, and more.

Veeck taught me the importance of making it fun every time you go to a game. So any time we could do an off-the-wall promo, I was ready to play. Over the years we've seen everything from singing pigs to wrestling bears to blind date nights. You name it, and we've tried it, as long as it was clean, legal, and moral. The best promotions are the ones you don't advertise in advance. You want your fans thinking, "What's going to happen tonight?"

I mentioned in our chapter on networking that I first met Bill Veeck by way of his book *Veeck, as in Wreck,* which told the story of his extraordinary life. Allow me to tell you something here about *my* life: I love books. It's really not much of a secret. You'll hardly ever see me without a book in hand. Let me just admit it: My name is Pat, and I'm a bookaholic. I love to read!

Books offer some of the most creative tools I can think of. Have you ever sat in a brainstorming session and watched the thoughts bounce off the walls? Well, books are like a personal brainstorming session. Just you and the author. She throws a few words on the page and suddenly your brain is in motion—recalling a time "when," or making a mental connection, or feeling a synapse fire with the brilliance of a fresh idea. Books help us discover how other people solved problems or innovated new products or developed cultural paradigm shifts. If you want to develop your own creativity—read!

Creativity over the years has been defined in many ways. One of the best (and simplest) definitions I've encountered is this: Creativity is the ability to have new thoughts. Mike Vance, the creativity expert who fathered "out of the box" thinking, offers another definition: "Creativity is the making of the new and rearranging of the old in a new way." I like Vance's definition because it recognizes both the birthing and nurturing elements of the creative process.

–MARK EPPLER, MOTIVATIONAL SPEAKER AND AUTHOR[41]

OPTIMISM IS ESSENTIAL

Nothing in this world is ever accomplished (*accomplish*: an adverb implying creativity) without a lot of persistence. Good old-fashioned sweat is what makes just about anything worthwhile happen. And the first ingredient in persistence is optimism: a belief in the best possible outcome. After all, if you don't believe that, why bother taking the next step? Most ideas die on the vine because people fail to persist. They get discouraged and their initial hopes and dreams fade.

Without a doubt, the Orlando Magic team exists today because of optimism. In the late 1980s, Orlando developer Jimmy Hewitt began dreaming of the day his growing town would have its own NBA team. He believed in his dream. He was optimistic that it could come true. So he contacted me, then general manager of the Philadelphia 76ers, and cast his vision. I bought in and the two of us got busy. We worked the town, talked up the team everywhere we went, convinced many locals to open their wallets, sold tickets, and eventually sold the NBA on our expansion team idea. Persistence doesn't begin to describe it. But Jimmy and I shared an optimistic, never-give-up streak. We saw that team before it was there. What dream can you make come true?

If you want to become more creative, you've got to find a way to tap into your own optimism. Maybe you've been on a mental downer for so long the ants know you by name. But I know you've still got it. It all goes back to that worldview we discussed earlier. Optimism is all about hope. It's been said that we can live three days without water, up to forty without food, but not one day without hope. Where is your source of hope? Find that, and you'll discover an endless fountain of creativity.

TIPS FOR STIMULATING CREATIVITY

In addition to being optimistic, or adopting an attitude of "yes," you can kindle your natural creativity by letting go of the need to be right all the time. Be willing to see the problem from all sides. This is especially important in the job interview arena.

If you're a creature of habit, as most of us are, try doing things a little differently from time to time. Wear your watch on a different wrist or sit in a new place at church or in the classroom. Read a book from a genre you haven't explored before. Listen to a different style of music. Doing familiar things in a different way is a great way to challenge your creativity.

Don't be afraid to waste time creatively now and then—at least on your own time. Not every employer appreciates this art form yet, but twentieth-century American author Wilferd Peterson, author of many books on wise living, did. He wrote, "Many times we will get more and better ideas in two hours of creative loafing than in eight hours at a desk."[42] Look at what companies like Pixar are producing, for example. You don't see those folks chained to workstations.

During your interview, find a way to let your creativity show. Wherever you've had success in the past, put it on parade—in a way that shows off your skills, not your ego. Today's companies value innovation. Their pool of employees is often where the depth of their reach begins.

> *Creativity can solve almost any problem.*
> *The creative act, the defeat of habit by*
> *originality, overcomes everything.*
>
> −GEORGE LOIS, ADVERTISING COMMUNICATOR

GoInnovate! founder Andrew Papageorge recognized this fact and has built his company on it. "Today more than ever, we must cultivate the creative and innovative potential of every employee in the organization," Papageorge has said. "Everyone in the organization must be capable of thinking creatively and be willing to try new approaches which transcend their own roles, departments and processes."[43]

So in the interview, display your sense of imagination. Let the interviewer know that you too value innovation. You may be asked about ideas you've come up with in the past that made a difference in your school, home, church, or workplace. Be ready to reveal your abilities as an idea person.

Retired CEO Jon Madonna has been quoted as saying, "Nothing stops an organization faster than people who believe that the way they worked yesterday is the way to work tomorrow." Whatever you do, don't get caught in that time warp way of thinking. Yes, Solomon himself, the wisest man who ever lived, said there is nothing new under the sun. And that may be true. But there are always new ways to apply anything you can imagine under the sun.

YOUR JOB INTERVIEW NAIL GUN: REVEAL CREATIVITY

1. Realize that you are a creative individual.

2. Come up with a few creative ways to express this side of your nature to the job interviewer.

3. Consider the portfolio. Once the domain of the artist or photographer, the portfolio today is not limited to examples of "art," but can offer a perspective on almost any area of expertise. Not sure how to develop one? What a great opportunity to explore your creativity!

4. Be optimistic. No matter what happens as a result of the job interview, something good has come from it. Whether or not you land this job, you have met new people, interviewed well, and learned more about yourself.

5. Let go of your need to be right and open yourself to new ideas. Become an idea encourager.

Don't Leave Home Without This Final Tip!

Every game has to have at least one free throw—so this one is mine. My final tip on nailing the job interview is the one likely to make the best impression of all:

BE YOURSELF!

Throughout this book we've offered practical pointers about making contacts, getting ready for the interview questions, dressing for success, communicating a solid message of integrity, and much more. As you consider all this advice, you might be feeling a little perplexed, as if you're not sure who that person is looking back at you from the mirror. Is that the polished professional or the creative genius? The party animal networker or the great communicator?

Here's the big idea: don't try to be any one of these qualities. Study them, wrap your mind around them, do your best to incorporate all of them into your life. But most of all, when you head into that interview you need to relax and just be you. Don't worry about competing with all those other folks, because when it comes right down to it, you can't. You are not like any of them, and none of them is like you. What you have to offer is singular, unique, and irreplaceable. You have yourself, and there is only one.

Robert Fulghum, author of *All I Need to Know I Learned in Kindergarten*, observes, "The statisticians figure that about 70 billion people have been born so far. And as I said, there's no telling how many more there will be, but it looks like a lot. And yet—and here comes the statistic of statistics—with all the possibilities for variation among the sex cells produced by each person's parents, it seems quite certain that each one of the billions of human beings who has ever existed has been distinctly different from every other human being, and that this will continue for the indefinite future.

"In other words, if you were to line up, on one side of the earth, every human being who ever lived or ever will live, and you took a good look at the whole motley crowd, you wouldn't find anybody exactly like you."[44]

One of my sports heroes, believe it or not, is not actually an athlete. I've long admired the man who is the legendary voice of the Los Angeles Dodgers—the great Vin Scully, now in his sixth Dodger decade and calling every game just as he sees them. Several years ago, I picked up a copy of *Investor's Business Daily* and read this great piece of advice Vin received early on from his mentor, the late great Baseball Hall of Fame announcer Red Barber: "Red said, 'Don't listen to other announcers. You can bring one special ingredient into the booth that no one else in the world can bring: yourself. There is nobody else in the world quite like you, so be yourself.'"[45]

When you go in for that job interview, think about Vin Scully. Walk in with confidence, fully aware that you're offering them one special component that no one else can offer. Be yourself!

Next time you're at church or school or in a movie theater, test it out. Look up and down the row. Isn't variety a wonderful thing? It proves that you are the only one who is just like you—a true designer original.

One thing my dad says is, "Be yourself. You are who you are. That's how you got here. Don't try to change or be something you're not."

–ELI MANNING, NEW YORK GIANTS QUARTERBACK[46]

THE TRUTH ABOUT YOU

So who are you? Have you asked yourself that question? All of us wonder at some time or another. The key is to figure it out and then be satisfied with the answer, because here's the truth about you: you are you, and the only you there is or ever will be. As author Oscar Wilde observed, "Be yourself; everyone else is already taken." We've noted this fact elsewhere in the book, but let's expand on it a little.

How can I be myself, you ask, *when I don't know who I am?* There is no doubt we live in a confusing time. Messages are bombarding us 24/7, telling us how we should dress, what we should smell like, what to eat followed by what eating it does to us, which workout equipment to use, what to take to help us sleep—it's enough to make anyone schizophrenic.

But it really isn't a mystery to figure out who you are. You just need to know the right questions to ask. So before you go into the job interview, take some time to interview yourself.

- What are you especially good at? If you're not sure, ask a few close friends for their honest assessment.

- What do you love to do? Or what would you love to learn more about?

- Who are you most passionate to help?

- If time and money were no object, what one thing would you do?

A person who knows his own dreams is more likely to be able to invest in the dreams of another. It's the old "it takes one to know one" principle. Employers love genuine, passionate people.

And in spite of what TV commercials or media ads try to tell us, everyone is drawn to the bold individual—the person who isn't afraid to be herself. She's not worried about fitting into a man-made mold, but easily expresses herself. The winning job candidate is most often relaxed and confident, comfortable in his own skin.

So when you go in for the interview, learn to flash that winning smile right off the bat. Find moments to laugh, have fun, and be relaxed. Demonstrate your natural sense of humor. No matter how much it hurts—look like you're having fun.

There's a great temptation when we're going for a big job to try to act like someone we are not—but that is always the wrong choice. Actress Judy Garland got it right when she advised, "Always be a first-rate version of yourself, instead of a second-rate version of somebody else." I couldn't have said it better.

Work hard. Be yourself. Do what you want to do. Do not follow the crowd.

–SAGAR PATEL, LODI HIGH SCHOOL
[NEW JERSEY] SENIOR[47]

WHAT IF I DON'T GET THE JOB?

If for some reason you don't get the job, remember it's not the end of the world. I like what I read about in a *Boston Globe* article on Harvard students learning to cope with rejection (yes, even Harvard students don't always get the job!): Harvard statistics professor Xiao-Li Meng began his two-page paper on rejection with the theorem, "For any acceptance worth competing for, the probability of a randomly selected applicant being rejected is higher than the probability of being accepted."[48] Very clever, and very true.

Not everyone gets on base every time they come up to bat. If I've learned nothing else in my career, it is that painful lesson. The *Boston Globe* article went on to make a point I definitely agree with: job candidates "should learn to see rejection as an opportunity to improve themselves, so that by the time they summon the courage to try again, they will be better candidates."

Earlier in this book we talked about the vision your life roadmap gives you to see where you're going. It's that kind of vision that can help you accept rejection. Sometimes we fail to get the job because we are not meant to win it—at least not now. Learn from the failure and try harder next time. Recognize that maybe *that* job, the one you just lost, would not have been the right one for you—no matter how much you wanted it. Or maybe the timing was not right.

I like what one writer I know has observed, "When my manuscript is rejected," she told me, "it's simply because I haven't found the right editor yet." That is so true! Personal chemistry has a lot to do with it, and we already know we don't "click" with everyone we meet.

So don't let it get you down if you don't get the job. Keep looking, keep interviewing, keep knocking on those doors. Be persistent. Don't give up! Continue to apply the principles in this book and in time the right door will open.

NAILING IT

What I'm getting at here—the lesson I hope you'll take with you—is that in order to *be* yourself, you first need to *see* yourself as you really are. Are you a hero? Many of us see ourselves in that way. But I believe the real heroes do not. If you've done heroic things, let the record speak for itself. Don't flaunt it, because as sure as you do, you can be certain you'll be shot down. Wait for it. Set your watch by it. It will happen.

By the same token, neither is anyone a complete zero. No matter how many times you've failed or what lies you've been told over the years, you are a person of great worth. After all, you are the one and only you. A Designer original—remember? No one else is like you and no one else has exactly what you bring to the table.

Life is not about your next job, or any job for that matter. If you are young, you may not realize that quite yet. If you are closer to the rocking chair than you want to admit, you already know that what I say is true—though you may have had to stumble upon it through a thorny path of failures and successes. Life is not about any job or career. It's about the person you become along the way.

An original is hard to find, but easy to recognize.

–JOHN MASON, INSPIRATIONAL SPEAKER AND AUTHOR[49]

The principles in this book are based on universal truths that, when applied, guarantee you will become a person of great character. While all of them encompass qualities job interviewers look for, none of them guarantees you will get that next job.

But Pat, you said this book is about nailing the job interview. What's with the rejection message? Yes, this book is about nailing the job interview and what I've offered is based on my own personal research into the qualities interviewers are looking for. Study them and apply them and your chances for success will be greatly improved.

But life doesn't follow any rulebooks. The only thing we can really be sure of is that things will change. As long as we draw breath, no situation is permanent. I believe, however, as literally billions have throughout history, that God's Word is true, and thousands of years ago, he promised: "For I know the plans that I have for you . . . plans to prosper you and not to harm you" (Jeremiah 29:11). If we hold fast to that promise, I believe we can weather any storm, any job loss, any disappointment, knowing that the whole story is not yet written.

So while none of these principles guarantees you will get the job, love the job if you do get it, or won't lose the job once you've found it, if you learn and apply them you will become a person others respect and admire, a person others want to be like.

And then you can share your story. Tell others how to nail the job interview, and better yet, how to live a worthwhile life—a life in which every moment counts.

Most of all, you'll be a person *you* can live with. At the end of the day, you'll be someone who sleeps well at night, knowing you've given that day and every day the best you had to give. That's what I call nailing it.

ABOUT THE AUTHOR:

Pat Williams

PAT WILLIAMS has been a leader in the world of professional sports for more than forty years. After many successful years as general manager of the Philadelphia 76ers, Pat helped found the NBA's Orlando Magic. He currently serves as that team's senior vice president.

One of the nation's leading motivational speakers, Pat has additionally authored over fifty-five books, including the popular How to Be Like series (Health Communications, Inc.).

Pat is passionate about inspiring positive life change, as his book titles reveal. Topics have ranged from biographies with practical application to marriage stability, parenting, building stronger teams, leading through servanthood, and more.

Most recently he has offered leadership wisdom in collaboration with Gene Griessman (*Lincoln Speaks to Leaders*, Elevate Books, 2009), life wisdom with his eldest daughter, Karyn (*The Takeaway*, HCI, 2009), and has challenged people to make every moment count in *What Are You Living For? Investing Your Life in What Matters Most* (Regal, 2009), written with Jim Denney.

In *Nail It!* Pat borrows from his lifetime of hiring experience to speak insight into the job interviewing process.

Pat and his wife, Ruth, live in Winter Park, Florida, where they are happy to be empty-nesters after raising nineteen children. They are both veterans of and experts at the job interviewing process and love to see people find the perfect professional fit.

Peggy Matthews Rose

PEGGY MATTHEWS ROSE is a writer who has partnered with Pat Williams on the books *Lincoln Speaks to Leaders* (with Gene Griessman, Elevate Books, 2009), *The Takeaway* (with Karyn Williams, HCI, 2009), *Read for your Life* (HCI, 2007) and *How to Be Like Walt*, written with Jim Denney (HCI, 2004). Her background reflects over twenty years with The Walt Disney Company, most of them in the communications field .

Other books she has worked on include *S.H.A.P.E.: Finding and Fulfilling Your Unique Purpose for Life*, by Erik Rees (Zondervan, 2006), *Only You Can Be You: 21 Days to Making Your Life Count*, also by Erik Rees (Howard Books, 2009), and the children's picture book *Tiffany and the Talking Frog in the Search for the Crown of Rye Chestnuts*, by Sandra Maddox (Triumvirate Publishing, 2008).

A leader with the Orange County Christian Writers Fellowship community, Peggy lives in Lake Forest, California, with her husband, Frank. Both have weathered numerous layoffs and job interviews and wish someone had given them a book like this one a lot earlier.

ACKNOWLEDGMENTS

With deep appreciation I acknowledge the support and guidance of the following people who helped make this book possible:

Special thanks to Bob Vander Weide, Rich DeVos, and Alex Martins of the Orlando Magic.

I'm grateful to my assistant, Latria Leak, who managed so many details that made this book possible. Thanks also to my writing partner, Peggy Matthews Rose, for her superb contributions in shaping this manuscript.

Hats off to three dependable associates—my trusted and valuable colleague Andrew Herdliska, my longtime adviser Ken Hussar, and my ace typist Fran Thomas.

Hearty thanks also go to my friend Adam Witty and his capable staff at Advantage Media Group. Thank you all for believing that we had something important to share and for providing the support and the forum to say it.

And finally, special thanks and appreciation go to my wife, Ruth, and to my wonderful and supportive family. They are truly the backbone of my life.

—PAT WILLIAMS

Special thanks to the following people
for their contributions to this book:

Gail Brown, Exceeding Expectations

Lorisse Garcia

Audra Hollifield

Ken Hussar

Maria Mancini

Brent Peterson, www.InterviewAngel.com

You can contact Pat Williams at:

Pat Williams

c/o Orlando Magic

8701 Maitland Summit Boulevard

Orlando, FL 32810

(407) 916-2404

pwilliams@orlandomagic.com

Visit Pat Williams' website at:

www.PatWilliamsMotivate.com

If you would like to set up a speaking engagement for Pat Williams, please call or Andrew Herdliska at 407-916-2401 or email him at aherdliska@orlandomagic.com.

We would love to hear from you. Please send your comments about this book to Pat Williams at the above address or in care of our publisher at the address below. Thank you.

Adam Witty

Advantage Media Group

P.O. Box 272

Charleston, South Carolina 29402

www.amglive.com

Resources used in compiling this book:

CHAPTER 1: NETWORKING

- http://interviewangel.blogspot.com/2009/04/easy-way-to-expand-your-network.html

CHAPTER 4: DISPLAY PROFESSIONALISM

- What does it mean to be a professional? http://findarticles.com/p/articles/mi_m0HUV/is_4_30/ai_81529255/
- http://www.tomreillytraining.com/Ezine%206-13-06%20ToBeaProfessional.htm
- http://www.auburnpub.com/articles/2008/03/14/lake_life/lakelife05.txt
- http://www.homebasedtrade.com/2007/august/professional.html
- How to dress tips sourced from http://www.fncimag.com/imag/ and http://jobsearch.about.com/od/interviewattire/a/interviewdress.htm

CHAPTER 6: EXHIBIT COMMUNICATION SKILLS

For help with cover letters and résumé preparation:
- http://jobsearch.about.com/od/coverlettersamples/a/coverlettsample.htm
- http://www.quintcareers.com/cover_letter_samples.html
- http://www.collegegrad.com/jobsearch/Best-College-Cover-Letters/Sample-Cover-Letter/
- http://www.bestcoverletters.com/
- http://www.rileyguide.com/cover.html
- http://office.microsoft.com/en-us/templates/CT101043371033.aspx
- http://www.landjob.com/Resume-Templates/
- http://docs.google.com/templates?q=resume
- http://www.easyjob.net/

Endnotes

CHAPTER 1: NETWORKING

1.   The Pursuit of Wow! Every Person's Guide to Topsy-Turvy Times, by Tom Peters (Vintage, 1994), p. 36

2.   Before the Committee On Energy and Commerce Subcommittee on Oversight and Investigations, United States House of Representatives, ¡Sexual Exploitation of Children Over the Internet: How the State of New Jersey is Combating Child Predators on the Internet." June 10, 2006, written testimony of Representative Michael G. Fitzpatrick, U.S. House of Representatives, eighth congressional district, State of Pennsylvania, p 2.

CHAPTER 2: BE INTERVIEW-QUESTION READY

3.   Deep Thoughts, by Jack Handey, Berkley Trade, 1992, p. 46.

CHAPTER 3: BE PREPARED

4.   http://pinetreeweb.com/bp-churchill.htm, from Great Contemporaries, by Winston S. Churchill (Thomas Butterworth Ltd, 1937).

5.   From "Jerry Rice announces retirement from football," by Eddie Pells of the Associated Press, USAToday, September 6, 2005. http://www.usatoday.com/sports/football/nfl/2005-09-05-rice-retirement_x.htm

6.   "New Rules for Landing a Job," by Bill Breen, Reader's Digest, February 2000.

7.   Ibid.

8.   Talent is Never Enough: Discover the Choices That Will Take You Beyond Your Talent, by John Maxwell (Thomas Nelson, 2007), p. 83

9. http://interviewangel.blogspot.com/2009/04/how-to-stop-fishing-at-job-fairs.html

CHAPTER 5: EXUDE SELF-CONFIDENCE

10. *Success* Magazine, February 2009, p. 56

11. "First year coach has Raiders winning his way," by Richard Weiner, USAToday, Pro Football, December 19, 2002. http://www.usatoday.com/sports/football/nfl/raiders/2002-12-19-callahan_x.htm

CHAPTER 6: EXHIBIT COMMUNICATION SKILLS

12. *Leading Change*, by John P. Kotter, Harvard Business Press, 1996, p. 9.

13. *Character in Action: The U.S. Coast Guard on Leadership*, by Donald T. Phillips and James M. Loy, Naval Institute Press, 2003, p. 71.

14. Posted April 14, 2009 by ChristianJobs.com

15. *Talk Like Jesus*, Lynn Wilford Scarborough, Phoenix Books, 2007, p. 3

16. http://tonyareiman.com/articles/body_language

17. *Building Character: Strengthening the Heart of Good Leadership*, by Gene Klann, Jossey-Bass, 2006, p. 136.

18. "Thanks for the Interview," by Sarah E. Needleman, *Wall Street Journal*, December 6, 2005.

19. "Interviewing is a Managerial Art," by Morey Stettner, Investor's Business Daily, October 24, 2005.

20. "Words That Get Your Hired," by Donald and Diana Stroetzel, Reader's Digest

21. *Leadership Secrets of the World's Most Successful CEO's: 100 Top Executives Reveal the Management Strategies That Made Their Companies Great*, by Eric Yaverbaum, Kaplan Business, 2004, p. 53.

CHAPTER 7: RADIATE ENERGY AND ENTHUSIASM

22. *Franklin and Winston: An Intimate Portrait of an Epic Friendship*, by Jon Meacham, Random House Trade Paperbacks, 2004, p. 14.

23. http://www.merriam-webster.com/dictionary/energy

24. http://www.foxnews.com/video2/video08.html?maven_referralObject=4538819&maven_referralPlaylistId=&sRevUrl=http://www.foxnews.com/americasnewsroom/

25. http://www.giantimpact.com/articles/read/article_influence_connecting_with_people/?utm_source=leadershipwired&utm_medium=email&utm_content=article&utm_campaign=lw-20090421

26. WordNet® 3.0. Princeton University. 22 Apr. 2009. <Dictionary.com http://dictionary.reference.com/browse/enthusiasm>.

27. *Jack Welch and the 4 E's of Leadership: How to Put GE's Leadership Formula to Work in Your Organizaion*, by Jeffrey Krames, McGraw-Hill, 2005, p. 25.

CHAPTER 8: REVEAL YOUR EXTRAVERSION

28. http://www.myersbriggs.org/my-mbti-personality-type/mbti-basics/extraversion-or-introversion.asp

29. http://ezinearticles.com/?How-to-Go-From-Introvert-to-Extrovert&id=99163

30. Interview Angel: Your Portable Guide to Getting Hired, pp. 2-10. www.InterviewAngel.com

31. http://www.giantimpact.com/articles/read/article_influence_ connecting_with_people/?utm_source=leadershipwired&utm_ medium=email&utm_content=article&utm_campaign=lw-20090421

CHAPTER 9: HAVE INTEGRITY

32. The Spurgeon Archive, Sermon No. 276, delivered September 25, 1859 at the Music Hall, Royal Surrey Gardens. http://www.spurgeon.org/ sermons/0276.htm

33. "The Qualities of Success," by R. Matthew Amboy, *Success* Magazine, May/June 2007, p. 53.

34. http://www.rbc.org/devotionals/our-daily-bread/2007/01/16/ devotion.aspx

35. *Character Makes a Difference: Where I'm From, Where I've Been, and What I Believe*, by Mike Huckabee with John Perry, B&H Books, 2007, pp. 98-99.

36. *What Made Jack Welch Jack Welch: How Ordinary People Become Extraordinary Leaders*, by Stephen H. Baum and Dave Conti, Random House, Inc., 2007, p. 17

37. *Thoughts of Chairman Buffett: Thirty Years of Unconventional Wisdom from the Sage of Omaha*, by Warren Buffett and Siimon Reynolds, Harper-Business 1998

Common Hiring Mistakes

38. Based on advice from Harvey Wigder, offered in Soft-Letter, January 17, 1995. http://www.allbusiness.com/human-resources/workforce-man- agement-hiring/486144-1.html

CHAPTER 10: REVEAL CREATIVITY

39. *The Imagineering Way*, by the Imagineers, Disney Editions, 2005, p. 24.

40. http://www.nigelpaine.com/articles/creativity-in-the-workplace/

41. *The Wright Way: 7 Problem Solving Principles That Can Make Your Business Soar*, by Mark Eppler, AMACOM, 2003, p. 106.

42. http://thinkersandjokers.com/thought.php?id=46901

43. *GoInnovate! A Practical Guide to Swift, Continual, and Effective Innovation*, by Andrew Papageorge, GoInnovate Publishing, p. 22.

CONCLUSION: DON'T LEAVE HOME WITHOUT THIS FINAL TIP

44. *All I Really Need to Know I Learned in Kindergarten*, by Robert Fulgham, Ballentine Books Revised Edition, 2004, p. 124.

45. "Vin Scully Brings His All To The Airwaves Follow Your Passion: Announcer's love of baseball, life and people have made him one of the best," by Michael Mink, Investor's Business Daily/LEADERS & SUCCESS, October 18, 2001.

46. http://www.quotesdaddy.com/quote/1281503/eli-manning/one-thing-my-dad-says-is-be-yourself-you-are-who-you

47. http://www.bookrags.com/highbeam/ambition-drives-math-whiz-fiction-19990509-hb/

48. "Accepting rejection: High-flying Harvard students get tips on how to rebound from the inevitagle 'thanks but no thanks,'" by Tracy Jan, *The Boston Globe*, Tuesday, April 21, 2009, pp. A1, A9.

49. *Know Your Limits—Then Ignore Them*, by John Mason, Insight International, 2000, p. 171

TreeNeutral

Advantage Media Group is proud to be a part of the Tree Neutral™ program. Tree Neutral offsets the number of trees consumed in the production and printing of this book by taking proactive steps such as planting trees in direct proportion to the number of trees used to print books. To learn more about Tree Neutral, please visit **www.treeneutral. com.** To learn more about Advantage Media Group's commitment to being a responsible steward of the environment, please visit **www. advantagefamily.com/green**

Nail It! is available in bulk quantities at special discounts for corporate, institutional, and educational purposes. To learn more about the special programs Advantage Media Group offers, please visit **www.KaizenUniversity.com** or call 1.866.775.1696.

Advantage Media Group is a leading publisher of business, motivation, and self-help authors. Do you have a manuscript or book idea that you would like to have considered for publication? Please visit **www.amgbook.com**

Printed in the USA
CPSIA information can be obtained
at www.ICGtesting.com
JSHW012035140824
68134JS00033B/3064